Comparable Worth

Also of Interest

The Underside of History: A View of Women Through Time, Elise Boulding

Women and Minorities in Science: Strategies for Increasing Participation, edited by Sheila M. Humphreys

Introduction to Library Research in Women's Studies, Susan E. Searing

Women in Third World Development, Sue Ellen M. Charlton

Working Women: A Study of Women in Paid Jobs, edited by Ann Seidman

New Spaces for Women, edited by Gerda Wekerle, Rebecca Peterson, and David Morley

International Law and the Status of Women, Natalie Kaufman Hevener

The Hidden Sun: Women of Modern Japan, Dorothy Robins-Mowry

Social Power and Influence of Women, edited by Liesa Stamm and Carol D. Ryff

*Available in hardcover and paperback.

A Westview Special Study

Comparable Worth: The Myth and the Movement
Elaine Johansen

"Comparable worth" has superseded "equal pay for equal work" as
the equal opportunity issue of the decade. On the ideological level,
it is a social doctrine that informs political action and portends
sweeping changes in defining the value of paid work traditionally performed by women. As a policy issue, it has achieved agenda-setting
value for political interest groups that wish to bring new evaluative
criteria to job assessment.

Professor Johansen traces the origins and development of the concept of comparable worth and analyzes its potential role in the economic advancement of women through political means. She looks at who
desires comparable worth and who does not, what standing it has in law
and legal precedents, and how its two "faces"--methodological and
ideological--are alternately used to enhance its development in the
public sector. Finally, she presents a policy framework for assessing
the economic and political basis for comparable worth's development
as a social doctrine, traces its diffusion through interest-group
strategies, and analyzes its probable consequences for the social
movement it represents and the institutions it is likely to affect.

Elaine Johansen is assistant professor of political science at
the University of Connecticut.

This book is dedicated to four people, each of whom contributed some special gift to the author. Two Floridians, Madeline S. Riffey, professor emeritus of the University of Miami, and Catherine Finegan (now deceased), citizen-activist of St. Petersburg, were both inspiring as friends and mentors: Madeline for her love of Florida and literature, Catherine for her vision of citizenship and devotion to politics. Since my tenure in Connecticut, I have received two other gifts: from the late Senator Audrey Beck, an appreciation of the vitality of life in politics dedicated to high principles; from Betty Seaver, editor and colleague, the encouragement to write.

Comparable Worth
The Myth and the Movement

Elaine Johansen

Westview Press / Boulder and London

A Westview Special Study

Portions of Chapter 3 are taken from "Social Doctrines to Implementation: The Case of Comparable Worth," which appears in *Policy Studies Review*, Summer 1984 issue.

This is a Westview softcover edition, manufactured on our own premises using equipment and methods that allow us to keep even specialized books in stock. It is printed on acid-free paper and bound in softcovers that carry the highest rating of NASTA in consultation with the AAP and the BMI.

Published in 1984 in the United States of America by Westview Press, Inc., 5500 Central Avenue, Boulder, Colorado 80301; Frederick A. Praeger, Publisher

Library of Congress Catalog Card Number: 84-51747

ISBN: 0-8133-0083-5

Composition for this book was provided by the author

Printed and bound in the United States of America

10 9 8 7 6 5 4 3 2

Contents

Tables and Figures

Acknowledgments

It's been not quite three years since an ironic comment sent me
unraveling a seemingly endless puzzle of what comparable worth represents as a policy issue. Comparable worth does not conform to the
rules of the game, but seems to create its own. Is it rulebreaking
or rulemaking, or is it a new game entirely? I wanted to inquire, to
question, and to construct and test theory without becoming a partisan
or a detractor. The people acknowledged here have helped me do that.
While I accept full responsibility for its content, this book would not
exist except for the persons named here. At the University of Connecticut, Larry Bowman, chair, Department of Political Science, suggested
the book, and colleagues George Cole, Robert Gilmour, Betty Hanson,
Everett Ladd, Carol Lewis, Norman Kogan, David RePass, Harold Seidman,
and Morton Tenzer offered support. Mark Daniels, Marilynn S. Dueker,
and Sarah Morehouse liberally contributed their assistance. Technical
assistance was gratefully received from G. Donald Ferree, Jr., Jack
E. Davis of the Institute for Social Inquiry, and Marilyn Penrod, art
director of the Division of Extended and Continuing Education. These
staff members of the Babbidge Library filled innumerable requests,
always with good humor: Robert Vrecenak, Isabelle DiCenzo, Scott
Kennedy, Ellen Embardo, Randall Jimmerson, and Cheryl Turkington.
Students Michael Burke, Laura Peck, Joseph Shurkus, and Nancy Tarkmeel
contributed references. Martha McCoy, doctoral candidate, and Betty
Seaver, copy editor, helped bring the manuscript to completion. The
University of Connecticut Research Foundation provided financial support. Elsewhere, Emoryette McDonald and James Parry contributed labor
relations expertise; N. Joseph Cayer, Philip Cook, Robert D. Fredlund,
L. Terrence Jones, and Mary Polci facilitated discussions in the early
stages of research. I am grateful, too, to the state directors of
personnel who generously responded to my survey.

E. J.

Introduction

AN OVERVIEW: THE POLITICS AND IMPLEMENTATION OF COMPARABLE WORTH

This book is about the evolution of a social doctrine called comparable worth that has sparked political debate about the value and character of women's work. Comparable worth challenges the dual occupation and wage structure for "male" and "female" jobs. Its two politically relevant dimensions are ideological and methodological. Ideologically, comparable worth informs political action and portends sweeping changes in definitions of the value of paid work traditionally done by women. Proponents see working women increasingly caught in a spiral of wage and status deflation, holding responsible jobs for less pay because they cannot be paired with "equal" but higher-paying job categories.[1] Until recent judicial rulings, the Equal Pay Act of 1963 and Title VII of the Civil Rights Act of 1964 have not offered women legal recourse to challenge sex-segregated occupations, market factors that may perpetuate inequity, or evaluation systems using factor weights that favor traditionally male occupations.[2]

The proponents of comparable worth propose a second look at traditional job evaluation. The methodology they sponsor assesses components of jobs relative to organizational purpose.[3] Additionally, it has agenda-setting value for groups who want to bring new evaluative criteria to job assessment through tactical interventions in personnel policies and procedures.[4]

The concept of comparable worth and its associated practices have given rise to policies and programs in the public sector for several reasons. There is increasing evidence that women's occupations are dominated by sex-segregated characteristics and wage differentials despite the Equal Pay Act of 1963 and Title VII of the Civil Rights Act of 1964. Second, there was consensus in

1

the feminist political community that the time had come
for a shift to economic issues, and that strategies to
attack sex bias in employment could be made politically
viable if organized and diffused nationally.[5] And, third,
coalitional politics directed more toward civil service
reform than sex-equity issues had potential for achieving
legislative, judicial, and administrative changes in
employment and wage structures because of the conflicting
mandates and practices of public personnel systems.[6]

The emergence of comparable worth is putting public
personnel administration in a classic policy dilemma:
Neither standing pat on traditional classification
systems nor initiating new evaluative practices will
shield it from legislative, union, or judicial
intervention.[7] Public personnel administration had
barely adjusted to the impact of the bilateral dimension
that collective bargaining brought to employee-management
relations in the 1970s[8] when a trilateral constituency of
administrative agencies and policymakers representing
women's groups and public-sector unions entered the
policy arena with an array of sophisticated
agenda-setting and implementation strategies, diffused
nationally,[9] to challenge existing systems.[10]

On the one hand the strategies reflect the
traditional use of public policies to assist the economic
advancement of women through pragmatic, incremental
tactics that focus on narrow role-equity issues to build
legislative support.[11] But the coalitions made important
additions: participation by affected groups in the
implementation of policies; and use of collective
bargaining and litigation to insure administrative
attention to the goals of the sponsors.

For comparable worth to have become a viable item on
the political agenda subnationally, three theoretically
important components had to be in place: (1) The
resources of the actors--the groups desiring change in
the economic status of women--had to conform to the
requirements of a pluralist, incremental decision
setting. They had to socialize the conflict within
manageable bounds by gathering allies and redefining the
issues. (2) The environment to be changed, i.e., the
public personnel system, had to be susceptible to the
displacement of conflict because of organizational
weakness. (3) The interest-group liberalism of lawmakers
and administrators had to give a prominent place in
implementation and oversight of program execution to
advocates.[12]

Regardless of the "mobilization of bias" in American
politics that had systematically limited the access to

power of women's groups, the knowledgeability and
structure of the feminist movement and its use of
pluralist ideology[13] gave it a decided advantage over the
managers and defenders of large public personnel systems.
Chronically underfunded and harnessed to piecemeal
systems that cover both merit principles and bargained
positions that are difficult to reconcile in practice,
public personnel administration is further hampered by
ideological confusion over whether its processes and
product are apolitical or not.[14] Whether administrators
accommodate to change or resist it depends on how they
see the nature of their work.

Policy goals for the advocates, on the other hand,
have remained fairly consistent irrespective of place.
The goals call for systemwide job evaluation studies, be
they for a city, state, or university system. Findings
of the studies could be used as the basis of follow-up
activities--perhaps sex discrimination suits under Title
VII of the Civil Rights Act of 1964, or negotiations
under merit systems or through collective bargaining for
equity adjustments, or classification and pay plan
revisions with employee, union, and women's advocacy
group participation.[15]

The story[16] of comparable worth[17] is essentially a
chronicle of the convergence of two powerful social
movements: the pay equity movement,[18] a spin-off or
cooptation of the women's rights movement of the 1960s,[19]
and the civil service reform movement of the late
1970s.[20] Each movement embodies a loose set of ideas
about societal needs, and each has fostered actions and
policy interventions that contain an identifiable
ideological nucleus.[21] The pay equity movement focuses on
the economic status of women; civil service reform, on
the deterioration of the managerial capacity of public
personnel administration and erosion of public confidence
in merit concepts. Both movements contain implicit
assumptions about structural elements of organizations
that affect strategies of change. Pay equity advocates
cite structural impediments to women's economic
progress,[22] treating the configuration of jobs, titles,
position hierarchies, salary schedules, and sex ratios
within and across occupations as significant determinants
of roles and behavior in organizations. This structural
emphasis has affected the definition of "discrimination"
as well; meaning has shifted toward the institutional and
systemic effects of structural exigencies, and away from
isolated, individual, or intentional wrongs.[23]

The civil service reform efforts of the late 1970s
similarly focused on structural remedies for
dysfunctional behavioral relationships.[24] Governments at

all levels reassigned responsibility and authority for
personnel decisions, separating adjudicatory and
executive functions and creating a managerial class with
its own conditions of employment to stem criticism of the
management of public affairs. The ethos of a
restructured public personnel management was to have been
professional, specialized services. The reality was
agencies operating in environments of political
turbulence and uncertainty, caught in conflict with
employees and outsiders who included legislatures,
unions, the media, other agencies, and interest groups.[25]

Several concerns guided the research reported here:
(1) What is comparable worth? Can it be defined? Can it
be applied? Where did it come from? Who wants it, and
who does not? (2) There is a wide range of activity in
the public sector having to do with comparable worth,
much centering on its use as an assessment methodology to
ferret out discriminatory potential in wage
differentials. Certainly the multitude of agenda-setting
and implementation strategies have functional
consequences. Who is advantaged by which strategies and
under what conditions? (3) Questions arise as to
whether there is a nonrandom diffusion pattern, which
might suggest innovativeness in states or localities or
particular strengths of organized interest groups. Does
the level of professionalism of state or local personnel
operations facilitate or retard the appearance of
comparable worth or its adoption and use? Or are policy
adoptions random, unattributable to political culture or
socioeconomic characteristics or regions? (4) Have
organized opponents arisen consistently or at all as
comparable worth gains legislative stature nationally?
Will power relationships shift as the issue becomes
redefined and more actors enter the power arena? Or will
actors, arenas of power, and relationships remain
consistent over time and from place to place?

Schattschneider believed that ordinarily it is the
weak who desire to socialize conflict. In that light,
the crucial problem in politics is the management of
conflict once an issue becomes salient. How the issue is
defined, and who is involved, the resources available,
and the displacement of conflict are all shifting
instruments of political strategy.[26]

It is assumed that how an issue is defined affects
the shape and outcome of conflict. The ability to define
an issue is a resource and depends on how specific or
abstract the issue is in objectives and symbolic
references, in its societal impact, and in its short-term
or long-term relevance. In addition the issue's
technical complexity and whether it is precedent setting

also act as contingencies that enhance or retard its development and diffusion. Some issues can be set in motion by unplanned events that are subsequently used as a resource by groups.[27] It is also assumed that mobilization of resources by social movement organizations differs from that of interest groups, particularly in defining issues with a societal impact.[28]

The research to follow will trace the origins and development of comparable worth as a concept and analyze its use and potential role in the economic advancement of women through political means. Chapters 1 and 2 review definitions and uses of comparable worth, who wants it, and who does not, and what standing it has in law or legal precedents. Chapter 3 explores how its two "faces"--methodological and ideological--are alternately used to enhance its development in the public sector.

The movement of comparable worth from principle to policies has depended upon the availability and use of symbolic and actual resources of the issue's sponsors during agenda setting and implementation, and the value structure or receptivity of the policy environment. Although coalitions tend to be the same regardless of locale--women officeholders, public-sector unions, and women's commission staffs--agenda-setting strategies have varied from open conflict to administrative remedies. Once into the implementation stage, however, it appears that both parties, advocates and administrators, find the bargaining and conflict to be to their partisan and mutual advantage.[29]

Chapter 3 constructs an analytic framework that (1) explains the development of comparable worth as an issue in public personnel administration, (2) accounts for why and how particularly critical events dramatically restructured political relationships and processes, and (3) offers a basis for prediction of future events.

The framework must account for the metamorphosis from interest-group phenomenon that pursued elite distributive policies concerned with study enactment to an administrative model of interaction concerned with the regulatory aspects of classification and pay. The framework must be flexible enough to account further for the emergence of mass-based support and opposition as elites try to manage the ramifications of the potential impact of the issue across class lines, and as the issue draws attention from the public.

Finally, Chapters 4 and 5 address the nature of changes sought, and where. Chapter 6 summarizes the economic and political basis for comparable worth's rise

as a social doctrine, traces its diffusion through
interest-group strategies, and analyzes its probable
consequences for the social movement it represents and
the institutions it will most probably affect.

NOTES

1. E. Johansen, "Managing the Revolution," Review
of Public Personnel Administration 4 (Spring 1984), p.
24.
2. E. Johansen, "From Social Doctrine to
Implementation," Policy Studies Review, Summer 1984,
forthcoming.
3. H. Remick, "Strategies for Creating Sound,
Bias-Free Job Evaluation Plans," paper presented at
Industrial Relations Counselors symposium, Atlanta,
September 1978.
4. Johansen, "From Social Doctrine to
Implementation."
5. E. Goodman, "Equal Pay for Work of Equivalent
Value," Washington Post, 21 May 1977, notes the change in
focus when she reports Ellie Smeal, president of the
National Organization for Women (NOW) as saying: "If our
basic goal is economic quality, if we are trying to
improve the economic conditions of the majority of the
American women, we have to start upgrading the jobs they
do."
6. E. Johansen, "Assessing the Comparable Worth
Controversy," Bureaucrat 13 (Spring 1984), p. 8.
7. E. Johansen, "Managing the Revolution," Review
of Public Personnel Administration 4 (Spring 1984), p.
26.
8. G.T. Sulzner, "Labor Relations with Public
Personnel Management," Policy Studies Journal 11
(December 1982), p. 280.
9. J. Grune, ed., Manual on Pay Equity (Washington,
DC: 1980).
10. Johansen, "From Social Doctrine to
Implementation."
11. J. Gelb and M.L. Palley, Women and Public
Policies (Princeton, 1982), pp. 9-12, distinguish two
kinds of issues: role equity and role change. "Role
equity issues are those policies which extend rights now
enjoyed by other groups. . . to women," issues that
appear narrow in their implication; "role change issues
are perceived to threaten existing dependent female roles
of wife, mother and homemaker."
12. T. Lowi, The End of Liberalism (New York, 1969),

p. 71, defines interest-group liberalism as an American
public philosophy that takes the pluralist notion that
government is an "epiphenomenon of politics" and expands
it to "what is good for government is good for society."
The good, or the public interest, can be defined in terms
of organized interests in society. Government, in this
view, is cast in a positive and expansive role,
redistributing opportunities and benefits, shaping
prosperity in society, and providing access to decision
making for the most effectively organized of interests.
Government's role becomes one of "ratifying" the
agreements worked out among the competing group leaders.

13. Gelb and Palley, Women and Public Policies, pp.
3-13.

14. D. Klinger, "Changing Role of Personnel
Management in the 1980s," Personnel Administrator
(September, 1979).

15. Johansen, "From Social Doctrine to
Implementation."

16. The policy analysis in this monograph assumes
the role of storytelling suggested by M. Rein, Social
Science and Public Policy (New York, 1979), to provide
competing views in matters of fact to enhance decisions
about value questions. The study of social policy in
Rein's view requires analysis of the interaction of
values, operating principles, and outcomes to be
productive. He suggests the study must include looking
at "how purposes and results relate to each other" and
"what dilemmas and consequences arise from trying to
implement conceptions of social justice or theories of
intervention" (p. 141). Hazards are multiple. Ideology
and beliefs attach themselves to both means and ends --
policy and outcomes -- and to the research about policy
as well. Social science contributes best to policy
debates by informing different ideological positions; it
cannot decide between the competing ideologies and be
persuasive. Social science can provide more objectivity
to the debate by injecting realism and a capacity for
effective action. Where there is a debate over factual
and normative questions and real conflict of moral
principles judged desirable by different standards, there
is opportunity for meaningful choice and a necessity for
sound advice. Advice giving, for Rein, is engaging in
storytelling from a value-critical perspective. Telling
relevant stories is valuable in that they can be accepted
irrespective of the disciplinal framework from which they
arise.

17. Comparable worth has assumed several identities
as its advocates and detractors have developed compatible
ideologies and labels to try to capture the momentum of
its effects on policies and publics. J. Freeman,
"Resource Mobilization and Strategy: A Model for
Analyzing Social Movements," in The Dynamics of Social

Movements, ed. M. Zald and J.D. McCarthy (Cambridge, MA, 1979), p. 167, notes that ideologies do not determine a movement's strategies but may emerge from actions and merely confirm or perhaps redirect them. Leaders of the pay equity movement appreciate this flexibility, moving away from comparable worth as it becomes encumbered with negative connotations, and embracing "pay equity," "objective job evaluation," or "equal value" as particular situations dictate. See testimony of Nancy Perlman, past chair of the National Committee on Pay Equity before the House Subcommittee on Compensation and Employee Benefits in Daily Labor Report, (Washington,DC: Bureau of National Affairs), no. 180, 16 September 1982, p. E6. See also remarks of Ruth G. Blumrosen, former consultant to the Equal Employment Opportunity Commission, 1965 to 1979, "Don't even say 'comparable worth,' it's losing language" (1981), as reported by L. Lorber and J. Kirk, "A Status Report on Comparable Worth," Public Personnel Management 12 (Winter 1983).

18. The pay equity movement fits the definitions offered in J. Gelb and E. Klein, Women's Movements: Organizing for Change in the 1980s (Washington, DC, 1983); J.R. Gusfield, ed. Protest, Reform and Revolt: A Reader in Social Movements (New York, 1970); and M. Ash, Social Movements in America (New York, 1972). Ash defines a social movement as a "set of attitudes and self conscious actions on the part of a group of people directed toward change in the social structure and/or ideology of a society and carried on outside of ideologically legitimate channels or which uses these channels in innovative ways" (p. 1).

19. The term "women's rights movement" is used to refer to those groups and organizations described by Carden, The New Feminist Movement (New York, 1974), that are pragmatic, atheoretical doers oriented toward using political processes and institutions to promote their concept of the rights and roles of women. Such groups make up the "feminist movement" depicted by Gelb and Palley, Women and Public Policies, pp. 1-12, as establishment actors committed to role equity issues, which center on extending rights enjoyed by other groups to women. The definition does not include general issue groups concerned about women included in Gelb and Klein's definition of women's groups (Women's Movements, p. 4), nor countermovement antifeminist organizations that use political institutions to effect social change. The women's rights movement is the "older branch" of what J. Freeman, in "Resource Mobilization and Strategy," in The Dynamics of Social Movements, ed. M. Zald and J.D. McCarthy (Cambridge, MA, 1979), called the women's liberation movement, and does not include organizations she terms "the younger branch." The latter group, which Carden calls "women's liberationists," like many

antifeminists organizations, concentrates a preponderance
of its attention on role-change issues rather than equity
issues. Gelb and Palley, Women and Public Policies, pp.
11-12, define role-change issues as those that appear to
"produce change in the dependent female role of wife,
mother, and homemaker, holding out the potential of
greater sexual freedom and independence in a variety of
contexts."

    20. Civil service reform is more than a social trend
but falls somewhat short of being an intensive
antiestablishmentarian social movement that uses
"collective action to bring about social change." J.R.
Gusfield, ed., Protest, Reform and Revolt (New York,
1970), p. viii. It best resembles Gusfield's description
of social movements that use reform as a model of change.
However the model of reform is not antiinstitutional,
romantic, or radical but, rather, institutional,
rationalistic, and bureaucratic. Like D. Moynihan's
example in "The Professionalization of Reform," in
Gusfield, Protest, Reform and Revolt, pp. 245-248, the
movement embodies a general strategy of professionally
executed reform. Where it departs from Moynihan is in
its focus on reforming government rather than society,
and its genesis within and outside government service.

    21. The definition of ideology used in this paper is
from G. Abcarian, "Political Defection and the Radical
Left," Journal of Social Issues 27 (January 1971), pp.
123-139, as "an integrated system of observations and
prescriptions that provides individuals with conceptual
basis for faith, evaluation, and action in life."
Radical ideologies share several mechanisms that enhance
what Abcarian terms the "faith maintenance" of the
holder. These include perceptual selectivity,
rationalization, normative certitude, and
transcendentalism. Both normative certitude, a "moral
sense of purity and validity" that derives from
commitment to an ideology, and transcendentalism, an
"ennobling sense of moral uplift," seem as common to
those supporting or opposing comparable worth as
perceptual selectivity and rationalization. One set of
adherents sees the issue as recouping women's place in
the economic system as individuals; the other sees the
issue as saving the free market system from disassembly
by a class-based interest. Both see government as the
supreme arbiter and resource for installing or
forestalling social change. See discussion by H.C.
Wagenaar of the impenetrable tangle of theories that
often form the ideological nucleus of policies, in D.B.G.
Kallen, et al., Social Science Research and Public Policy
Making (London, 1982), pp. 26-27.

    22. R. Kantor, "Presentation VI," in Women and the
Workplace, ed. M. Blaxall and B. Reagan (Chicago, 1976),
p. 287; R. Steinberg, "Typical and Alternative Routes to

Promotion of Women and Minorities," _Journal of Public and International Affairs_ 3 (Fall/Winter 1982).

23. Steinberg, "Typical and Alternative Routes to Promotion," p. 13; Senate Rep. No. 92-415, 92d Cong., 1st sess. 5 (1971); D. Stewart, "Managing Competing Claims: An Ethical Framework for Human Resource Decision Making," _Public Administration Review_ 44 (January/February 1984), p. 16; J. O'Neill, "Women and the Labor Market," in House Subcommittees on Human Resources and Civil Service Compensation and Employee Benefits of the Committee on Post Office and Civil Service, _Pay Equity Hearings, September 16, 21, 30 and December 2, 1982,_ 97th Cong., 2d sess., 1982.

24. C. Bellone, "Structural vs. Behavioral Change: The Civil Service Reform Act of 1978," _Review of Public Personnel Administration_ 2 (Spring 1982), p. 59.

25. Klinger, "Changing Role of Personnel Management in the 1980s," p. 42.

26. E.E. Schattschneider, _The Semisovereign People_ (Hinsdale, IL, 1960), pp. 36,40,69,170.

27. R.W. Cobb, and C.D. Elder, _Participation in American Politics_ (Boston, 1972), pp. 96-102.

28. Freeman, "Resource Mobilization and Strategy," p. 172.

29. M. Collett, "Comparable Worth: An Overview," _Public Personnel Management_ 12 (Winter 1983), p. 325.

1
Why Comparable Worth?

DEFINITIONS AND CONTEXT

Comparable worth is a controversial concept. Some say it cannot be operationally defined now or ever,[1] others define and use it.[2] Some insist that women's wages are a result of their own choice of, or "investments" in, education, training, and roles; that women choose jobs that allow them to enter and leave the labor market easily to complement their roles as wives and mothers.[3] Women thus lack marketable skills, are not part of a competitive labor market, and are concentrated in a narrow band of small-pay occupations[4] labeled "women's work."[5] Still other commentators assert that women have always worked;[6] have invariably been sex segregated into menial or low-status occupations; are victims of pervasive, systematic, institutionalized discrimination in employment; and until very recently have had no legal or political remedy.[7]

The arguments of economists over the possible interactive effect that training, skills, continuity, and longevity have on women's occupational choice, productivity, and pay devolve to circular defenses of particular economic theories: human capital versus stratified or dual-market models. Although the labor market participation of women escalated dramatically in the postwar years, statistics continue to attest no change in the relative earnings of men and women.[8]

To explain the persistence of the pay differential between jobs held mainly by women and jobs held mainly by men, a select committee of the National Research Council of the National Academy of Sciences (NAS) commenced a three-year study in 1978 commissioned by the Equal Employment Opportunity Commission. The NAS committee considered to what extent discrimination accounted for

11

12

the gap in earnings, and whether any remedy was
possible.[9] It reviewed the evidence on the extent of
wage differentials, concluded that there was a
substantial difference in earnings between men and women,
and addressed the complex set of forces reflected in
labor markets and institutional contexts that affected
wage administration practices.

/ The NAS research indicated that such factors as
labor market segmentation, job segregation, and
employment practices permitted the persistence of
earnings differentials between men and women.[10] The
committee discounted the idea that job segregation might
be due only to women's choice. It concluded that
although some women do choose low-paying jobs that permit
dropping in and out of the labor market, job segregation
also "results from the exclusionary practices of
employers and from the systematic underpayment of jobs
held mainly by women."[11] The committee proposed that
there be renewed development of job evaluation tools with
special attention to their use in identifying and
correcting any inadvertent bias, and experimentation with
new procedures to remove bias statistically, if
present.[12]/

The principal investigators for the committee,
Treiman and Hartmann, later reiterated these conclusions,
stating that comparable worth "arises because of the
large and continuing differential in men's and women's
earnings and the persistent segregation of men and women
in the labor market."[13] The final committee
recommendations of the NAS had been foreshadowed by the
first-year interim report in 1979 authored by Treiman.
He had sought to "determine whether appropriate job
measurement procedures existed or could be developed to
assess the worth of jobs."[14] He defined such
measurement, commonly called job evaluation, as referring
"to a formal procedure for hierarchically ordering a set
of jobs or positions with respect to their value or
worth, usually for the purpose of setting pay rates."[15]

SIGNIFICANCE OF JOB EVALUATION

Although job evaluation had its origins in the early
time-and-motion studies developed by the father of
scientific management, Frederick W. Taylor, in 1881,
management did not begin to attend to the capability of
the analysis of jobs to increase productivity and
decrease cost until after the publication of Taylor's
Shop Management in 1911.[16] Municipalities, banks, and
industries began using job analysis to evaluate positions
and set wages. World War I sparked an upsurge in the
"new movement" of personnel management, and there were at

least four methods of evaluating jobs by 1926.

Two congressional measures in the 1930s hastened the adoption of job evaluation: the National Labor Relations Act of 1935 (the Wagner Act), which business viewed as favorable to labor groups; and the Fair Labor Standards Act of 1938, which set minimum wages for specified groups. The former established the principle that employees had the right to organize into labor unions and to bargain collectively on wages and working conditions; the latter necessitated proper classifications of employees.[17] The greatest incidence of job evaluation plans in government and the private sector occurred during and after World War II, further stimulated by the War Labor Board and by the Treasury Department's "Rules on Salary Schedules." The Treasury Department rules applied to all salaried workers earning over $5,000; the national War Labor Board had jurisdiction over all wage earners.[18]

Organized labor reportedly was distrustful and suspicious of job evaluation techniques in the 1940s, criticizing them as "being subject to the element of human judgment and consequently subject to the bias and prejudice of those who are installing and maintaining them." Advisers to business cautioned that it was "to be expected that unions would be slow in giving their support," but promoted job evaluation as an attempt to "determine the worth of each job in relationship to the worth of all other jobs."[19] They cited two primary benefits: job evaluation provided a framework for policy determination, and eliminated pay inequities caused by favoritism or undue pressure.[20]

So it was that the dual desires of organizations to gain control of differentiating and classifying content of work according to its value, and to remain autonomous in those decisions from outside pressure by unions or government led to the early institutionalization of job evaluation practices of each organization's or consultant's own design. By 1955 job evaluation was a widely used management technique in place well before the bulk of civil rights legislation of the 1960s.

Treiman observed that by the mid-1950s interest in job evaluation as a research topic had ebbed.[22] It reportedly was of small concern to practicing psychologists and academics. Like employment testing, job evaluation had gone through several quiet decades of unquestioned use, and was undoubtedly vulnerable to legal challenges relating to validity, documentation, administrative use, and equity.[23] It is in this atmosphere that comparable worth and the debate over wage

rate differentials and sex-segregated occupations of
women was to take root.

OPERATIONAL DEFINITIONS OF COMPARABLE WORTH

What is comparable worth?   Can it be operationally
defined?

Comparable worth had its origins in the peace treaty
negotiations after World War I that established the
International Labour Organization. The phrase "equal pay
for work of equal value" was used then and in subsequent
international conferences in 1951,   1957, and 1975, to
urge   member   nations   to put   the philosophy   into
practice.[24] Acceptance was slow,   and in some countries,
nonexistent,[25] but in the United States since 1975 it has
taken on the character of a social movement,[26] and there
is renewed activity in Congress.[27]

Comparable worth is a concept that encourages an
organization   or   community   to   express   the   value   it
attaches   to   components   of   jobs   by   identifying   and
weighting various factors--such as knowledge and skill,
accountability,   and   working   conditions--so   that
relationships   between job   content and wages are   made
explicit and comparisons can be made.   Jobs are ordered
hierarchically   through   job   evaluation   procedures   and
grouped according to pay classes.

Job evaluation undertaken in the public sector to
emphasize comparable worth goals is similar to,   yet
different from,   conventional job evaluation practices.
Its similarity is that it employs the traditional tools;
it first surveys and verifies descriptions of each job,
then numerically weights component factors according to
complexity or worth.   Its dissimilarities are threefold.
The   first   is   the   level   of   scrutiny   accorded   job
descriptions,   factors,   and factor weights.   Evaluation
teams are specifically trained to sensitize them to sex
bias in job analysis.   The second difference is the
weighting   of   factors   to   complement   organizational
purpose.   The third difference is in the deployment of
the evaluation teams as technical advisers to advisory
committees--whose   members   are   appointed   from   labor,
women's organizations,   management,   and business--that
make   policy   recommendations   to   legislative   and
administrative bodies.[28]

While none of these practices alone can insure
against   the   potentially   problematic   aspects   of   job
evaluation   identified   by   Treiman--the   sensitivity   of
analysis to the choice of compensable factors and their
weights,   and the inherently subjective judgments about

job content--together they contribute a greater measure of control over sex bias.[29] Participants build a hierarchy of job classes by first defining a set of factors that are assumed, "a priori," to be contributors to the value of jobs. This building process is employed in lieu of using "policy-capturing" techniques that merely generate factors from statistical analysis of the current wage hierarchy. Existing hierarchies are thought to include unexamined bias within their factors and are therefore avoided. Through the rigor of their study and discussions, evaluation teams define and weight factors, adding a dimension to a technical process that reportedly is perceived by employees as "fair, systematic and credible."[30]

Three senior officers of Hay Associates, a management consulting firm with long tenure in job evaluation, report implementing comparable worth vehicles in hundreds of private-sector firms. They note that comparable worth has been implemented for large heterogeneous populations only through legislation for government employees. On the basis of their experience they suggest that comparable worth works where employees understand the institutional culture, there is substantial homogeneity of values, and the employees "accept the value system implied by the job evaluation methodology."[31]

In general, all economic organizations and communities that hire people are characterized by value systems that implicitly or explicitly determine "the relative importance of job and individual characteristics in determining salaries."[32] The value of comparable worth lies in its diagnostic potential as a policy tool. It graphically reveals how payment per unit of content, or relative value, is distributed across a hierarchy of jobs that have been rank ordered by their relative importance to the organization. Its purpose is to show where sex-based pay differentials exist for positions in which one sex or another predominates.

There is nothing metaphysical about comparable worth. Nor is it any more technocratic than customary job evaluation. It is not necessarily radical or hostile to a market system. It is, however, an inherently political process by virtue of its development in the public sector through lobbying, collective bargaining and litigation, and the use of joint labor-management teams to identify criteria of worth used to construct relationships between job size and pay.[33]

POLITICIZATION OF PUBLIC PERSONNEL

Comparable worth cannot be defined apart from the
social institutions that have shaped its meaning and
expression. A largely unnoted struggle to change the
quality, representativeness, and level of performance of
public personnel systems, civil service reform, was to
have a far-reaching effect on how comparable worth was to
be operationalized in the public sector at all levels.
The federal reform activities generally followed rather
than preceded major reorganizations of personnel
administration in more than thirty states and hundreds of
cities.[34] Yet the changes sought--"to improve employee
performance, to increase accountability to elected
officials, to allow managers more discretion,...to
achieve a work force that includes more women,
minorities, and handicapped in higher positions,"[35] and
to give statutory status to collective bargaining--were
strongly resisted by employees of the federal and state
governments. Conflict between standpatters and those
desiring change helped to politicize the reform
legislation when it was considered, and the practice of
personnel administration for some time after.

The 1978 Civil Service Reform Act for the most part
was patterned after state government reforms of the early
1970s and represented a thoroughgoing structural
reorganization of federal personnel administration. The
Civil Service Commission was replaced by the Office of
Personnel Management (OPM), with authority for human
resource management, and the Merit Systems Protection
Board (MSPB) to oversee appeal functions and review OPM
rules and regulations. A prime reason for the overhaul
was to strengthen eroded merit principles and protections
that had been highlighted during the Watergate era.[36]
Prominent among the merit principles in the act was a
provision dealing with comparable worth: "Equal pay
should be provided for work of equal value with
appropriate consideration of both national and local
rates paid by employees in the private sector."[37]

Alan Campbell, chairman of the U.S. Civil Service
Commission testified on behalf of the Carter
administration in support of the Civil Service Reform Act
and Reorganization Plan No. 2 of 1978.[38] He described
complaints of inadequate protection from partisan
pressures, layers of controls and procedures, and lengthy
appeal processes that had led to intensive study by nine
task forces. Their mission was to recommend improvements
in the roles, functions, structure, and effectiveness of
public personnel management. Their report focused on two
central challenges to personnel management: the necessity
for a stronger foundation for both the protection of

employee rights and the application of the merit concept, and the development of new approaches to personnel operations and administration.[39]

This was not the first time that threats to merit principles had been raised as an issue underlying criticism of the operation of public personnel systems. Merit principles that kindled the Pendleton Act and the first civil service reform in the 1880s had been "born of a reform ideology" that wished to correct the abuses of patronage and insure that the most qualified were selected for public service.

In the 1970s a second push for reform gained momentum. Public affairs journals were replete with complaints about merit's loss of effectiveness as a standard in personnel administration and the existence of a "meritless" civil service system.[40] Empirical evidence began to accumulate that the discussion of the tenuous nature of merit systems was more closely related to opposition to the "twin threats" of affirmative action and collective bargaining. While many personnel administrators supported in principle the notion that minorities and women should not be discriminated against, giving preference to them in personnel actions was resisted.[41] Similarly, many objected to bilateral negotiations between management and organized public employees, seeing the negotiations as a further threat to merit principles.[42] The advent of public-sector collective bargaining brought increased pressure to expand its scope to include union participation in decisions formerly held to be management prerogatives. Additionally, it created a bilateral relationship between management and the unions--the new advocate and exclusive employee representative.[43]

POLICIES OF STATE AND FEDERAL GOVERNMENTS

Activity surrounding the Civil Service Reform Act of 1978 that occurred coincident with governmental reorganization at the federal level signaled profound discontent with the civil service system in general and the operation of Equal Employment Opportunity Commission in particular. Both acts were conceived within the Carter administration and were to have an effect on support for comparable worth.

The Civil Service Reform Act instigated dramatic change in government personnel systems. Symbolically, it included the concept of comparable worth or equal value in the nine basic merit principles. The second change, Reorganization Plan No. 1 of 1978, was to have a direct impact on the practices associated with comparable worth.

The plan to reorganize the Equal Employment Opportunity Commission (EEOC) was presented in July 1977 by Eleanor Holmes Norton, less than sixty days after her confirmation as its head. The plan transferred federal equal employment functions from the Civil Service Commission to the EEOC, effective January 1979.

The reorganization of EEOC exampled leverage of those actors with inside access to administrative agencies. This phenomenon is repeated often in the story of comparable worth. Reorganization Plan No. 1 provided the institutional base for EEOC's commissioning of the National Academy of Sciences (NAS) three-year study of job evaluation, and other support that enabled identification of test cases for litigation of comparable worth.

From 1965 when the EEOC was created until 1977 it had had eleven chairpersons and had been seriously undermined by lack of continuity of policy, evidenced in contradictory lower court rulings. There was a backlog of 130,000 cases when Norton arrived, complaints of inadequate information systems, and lack of coordination between investigatory and litigation functions in the agency. The Supreme Court in 1981 noted EEOC's inconsistent policy guidelines for interpreting the Bennett Amendment, and a General Accounting Office study confirmed that serious dysfunctions hampered its fulfillment of its mission.[44]

EEOC had been established by Title VII of the Civil Rights Act of 1964 to seek out and eliminate unlawful employment practices. It was initially given power only to investigate and conciliate charges of discrimination, but in 1972 was authorized to file suit in federal district court when it believed an employer was engaged in a pattern or practice of discrimination. Organizational accommodations to the litigation responsibilities added in 1972 were layered-in structurally, creating a haphazard effect on the agency's mission.

Norton's reorganization streamlined and integrated the litigation structure so that all field offices could engage in charge processing. She created the Office of Policy Implementation to guide commissioners in making policy, and the Office of Government Employment to facilitate development of antidiscrimination programs for state and local governments. EEOC would be responsible for investigating and enforcing Title VII of the Civil Rights Act of 1964[45] and Title VII, as amended by the Equal Employment Opportunity Act of 1972,[46] through its reorganized twenty-two district offices and forty-six

area offices. EEOC responsibilities also included
providing coherence and direction to the government's
equal opportunity efforts under Executive Order 12067 of
30 June 1978; enforcement in private industry as well of
the Equal Pay Act of 1963 commencing in July 1979; and
the Age Discrimination in Employment Act of 1967 (ADEA).

An attorney by training, and former administrator of
New York City's Commission on Human Rights, Norton was
enthusiastically described by senators of both parties in
the confirmation hearings as a "woman whose time has
come" to take on a job "that has been waiting" for her.[47]
Her breadth of experience allowed her to focus on the
organizational impediments to establishing aggressive
pattern and practice surveillance and the development of
consistent and integrated policies. She envisioned that
reorganization presented "a magic opportunity for civil
rights efforts in government," which had been dissipated
by having "civil rights machinery...flung across the
entire government." In her judgment, "pattern and
practice cases alone /could/ have impact /affecting/
discrimination of millions of minorities and women...."[48]

Gifted in persuasion and presence, Norton
appreciated qualities that exhibited "principled ideology
that was never waylaid by faddishness."[49] Her plan was
both idealistic and pragmatic: to consolidate the
organizational capacity of the EEOC. Two consultants to
the commission from Rutgers University were particularly
helpful in this regard: Alfred Blumrosen, instrumental
in the design of reorganization, and Ruth Blumrosen,
author of law review articles that became the centerpiece
of early legal scholarship on comparable worth.[50] Alfred
Blumrosen saw the reorganization as a chance to allow the
commission "to concentrate on systemic discrimination."[51]
Ruth Blumrosen's scholarly work helped to broaden the
dialogue concerning the Bennett Amendment and to
reconcile the Equal Pay Act and Title VII. In October
1979, Norton announced her intention to hold public
hearings "to examine the nature and present extent of job
segregation, the relationship between job segregation and
wage differentials, and how segregation may adversely
influence the setting of wages for segregated jobs."[52]
The hearings were instrumental in generating momentum for
discussion and action related to comparable worth.

BREAKTHROUGH WITH GUNTHER

Comparable worth's first practical application in
the public sector was by the State of Washington, which
began a job evaluation study in 1973. The state used a
point-factor job evaluation system to assess the extent
of sex-related differences for a selected group of

sex-dominated positions in the state civil service. Consultants Norman D. Willis and Associates, surveyed one hundred twenty-one positions that were characterized by over 70 percent incumbency by one sex. Thirteen state employees and representatives of public unions, private businesses, and women's groups were trained as evaluators of job content based on factors of knowledge and skills, mental demands, accountability, and working conditions. The study demonstrated substantial underpayment: 25-35 percent for female employees in job classes requiring the same level of skill, effort, and responsibility as predominantly male classifications. The report exhibited a "policy line" on a scattergram that enabled comparisons of an array of the actual and predicted job worth scores and salaries for selected classifications.

The State of Washington declined to implement the study and commissioned two updates, one in 1976 and another in 1980. Both later studies corroborated the original findings. Continued nonimplementation, the statutory prohibition against bargaining over wages, and the Gunther decision sent the American Federation of State, County and Municipal Employees (AFSCME) to court.[53]

The AFSCME suit against the State of Washington was initiated following the landmark U.S. Supreme court ruling in County of Washington v. Gunther, June 1981. The court held that a provision that had been appended to Title VII, the Bennett Amendment, did not limit Title VII's prohibition against sex-based wage discrimination to claims of equal pay for equal work, as several lower courts had previously ruled. Rather, by a five-to-four vote, the court affirmed another lower court decision in Gunther that Title VII plaintiffs do not have to prove that jobs they hold are substantially equal to sustain a claim of wage discrimination under Title VII. The court found ample support for inference of intentional discrimination in the employer's disregard of the employer's own evaluation of male and female jobs: men were being paid 100 percent of evaluated worth, and women 30 percent less.[54] Although the court acknowledged the scholarly interest in comparable worth, it specifically stated that evidence supporting the concept, standing alone, was insufficient to establish a prima facie case of sex-based wage discrimination.[55]

PRESSURE FOR CHANGE

Gunther changed the legal framework within which proponents would develop their strategies. For years the majority of courts had interpreted the Bennett Amendment as having incorporated the "equal pay for equal work"

standard of the Equal Pay Act into Title VII.[56] By
holding that a course of action for sex discrimination
could be "brought under Title VII without satisfying the
equal work standard of the Equal Pay Act,"[57] the court
made finding evidence sufficient for a Title VII claim a
high and certain goal for advocates. Comparable worth
studies would become a vehicle to dramatize gender-based
wage disparities, or to support suits charging
discrimination. The ruling became an indispensable tool
in a growing and diverse arsenal.

The period between 1973, when the Washington study
commenced, and 1982, when AFSCME filed suit, witnessed
the diffusion of the idea of comparable worth as the
focus of political activity and the spread of conditions
necessary for its growth and adoption. Chapter 2 deals
with the historical progression of how the pay equity
movement arose from the postwar feminist movement to plan
and induce change by establishing linkages between
critical policy actors and groups. The activities were
engendered by the profound discontent with state and
federal laws and practices among ever-broadening networks
of women, some as "insiders" in government.

Many social theorists concerned with social
movements find such movements arise from discontent with
institutions and their rules, or other social controls.
Social movements, despite their origins, become
collective actions to demand change, and exist in a
political and ideological context. Movement members
share a general perception of what is wrong and what
should be done about it.[58]

Social movements garner resources from
beneficiaries, sympathizers, and institutions whose
resources are potentially cooptable if mobilized. The
most obvious source of cooptation is government.[59] Laws
and institutions of government determine power
relationships between and among groups and are therefore
prime targets for those desiring social change. Freeman
notes that laws against discrimination, for instance,
moved civil rights advocates from sit-ins to the courts.
Before Title VII, the numbers of supporters were
important to dramatize discrimination; after, attorneys
were important. Before Title VII, legislatures were the
battleground; after, the courts.

A major factor, then, in consolidating advantages of
institutional cooptation is the appropriate vehicle:
numerous supporters and access to decision makers when
seeking legislation; or specialized expertise when
defending legislative gains. The occasion must
complement the use of resource, and vice versa. Enormous

costs are attendant upon the mobilization of aggrieved
individuals and groups, so their ready identification and
relative density--that is, how concentrated or scattered
they are--are prime considerations.[60]

The remarkable changes wrought by the Civil Service
Reform Act and Reorganization Plans 1 and 2--symbolically
referencing equal value as an integral part of basic
merit system principles, instituting collective
bargaining in federal service by statute where it
formerly existed by executive order, decentralizing
personnel operation, and streamlining the decision-making
capabilities of the EEOC--all set off reverberations of
conflict. Those who supported the status quo would
resist. Those who had sought change would try to
consolidate their gains in real power.

Comparable worth would arise as the EEO issue of the
1980s. Its use as a way to broaden conventional job
evaluation techniques in public jurisdictions to reduce
bias would be tested. Its standing in law would receive
serious consideration. So, too, the numerous studies
that would investigate gender-based wage disparities.
Structural changes in personnel administration and EEOC
would accelerate comparable worth policies and studies.
Rising expectations would become more pronounced among
working women in the public sector.

How did this situation arise? Why in the public
sector? What precedent does it have in the history of the
political intervention of women in politics? What groups
or individuals constitute the movement? Where did it all
begin, and where will it end?

NOTES

1. E.R. Livernash, *Comparable Worth: Issues and
Alternatives* (Washington, DC, 1980), p. 8.
2. U.S. District Judge Jack E. Tanner uses the
definition of the defendant in *American Federation of
State, County, and Municipal Employees* v. *The State of
Washington*, Docket No. C 82-465T, as "the provision of
similar salaries for positions that require or impose
similar responsibilities, judgments, knowledge, skills,
and working conditions." *Daily Labor Report* (Washington,
DC: Bureau of National Affairs), 15 December 1983, p.
D-7. Tanner ruled that the State of Washington had
engaged in intentional sex discrimination in violation of

Title VII of the Civil Rights Act of 1964 as amended.
   3.   For arguments favoring this point of view, see
Livernash, Comparable Worth, and an untitled paper
delivered by economist June O'Neill at International
Personnel Manager's Association National Conference,
Washington, DC, October 1983.   For summary of literature
on sex-role socialization, see P. England, M. Chassie,
and L. McCormack in "Skill Demands and Earnings in Female
and Male Occupations," Sociology and Social Research 66
(January 1982), pp. 147-48.   For analysis of
intermittancy of women's labor force participation, see
ibid., pp. 148-68; and W. Wolf and R. Rosenfeld, "Sex
Structure of Occupations and Job Mobility," Social Forces
56 (March 1978), pp. 823-44.
   4.   For a discussion of the costs of sex-segregated
labor markets see A.W. Niemi, Jr., "Sexist Earnings
Differences: The Cost of Female Sexuality," American
Journal of Economics and Sociology 36 (January 1977), pp.
33-40, and testimony of Commissioner Janet Norwood,
U.S.Bureau of Labor Statistics in Joint Hearings on Pay
Equity: Equal Pay for Work of Comparable Value, Part I
and II, 97th Cong., 2d sess. Hereafter cited as Pay
Equity.
   5.   V.K. Oppenheimer, The Female Labor Force in the
United States: Demographic and Economic Factors Governing
Its Growth and Changing Composition (Westport, CT, 1970),
covers many of these issues.   For a cogent discussion of
sex labeling and segregation of jobs see especially ch.
3, pp. 60-120.
   6.   J.W. Scott, "Mechanization of Women's Work,"
Scientific American, September 1982, pp. 166-87.
   7.   R. Blumrosen, "Wage Discrimination, Job
Segregation and Title VII," University of Michigan
Journal of Law Reform 12 (Spring 1979), pp. 397-502,
surveys much of the literature.
   8.   National Research Council press release, "Women
Still Earn Less," 1 September 1981, pp. 1-4.
   9.   See committee report in D. Treiman and H.
Hartmann, Women, Work and Wages (Washington, 1981).
   10. Ibid, p. 11.
   11. National Research Council press release, "Women
Still Earn Less," p. 2.
   12. H. Hartmann and D. Treiman, "Notes on the
National Academy of Sciences Study of Equal Pay for Jobs
of Equal Value," in Public Personnel Management Journal
12 (Winter, 1983), p. 404.
   13. Ibid.
   14. D. Treiman, Job Evaluation: An Analytic Review
(Washington, 1979), p. xi.
   15. Ibid., p. 1.
   16. See history and bibliographic references in E.
Lantham, Job Evaluation (New York, 1955), pp. 6-12.
   17. Ibid.

18. C.W. Lytle, Job Evaluation Methods (New York, 1946), pp. 298-314. For an extended discussion of War Labor Board action relative to comparable worth, see R. Blumrosen, "Wage Discrimination, Job Segregation, and Women Workers," p. 47; R.E. Williams and D.S. McDowell, "The Legal Framework," in Comparable Worth: Issues and Alternatives, ed. E.R. Livernash (Washington, DC: 1980), pp.214-15; and B.A. Nelson, E.M. Opton, and T.E. Watson, "Wage Discrimination and the 'Comparable Worth' Theory in Perspective," University of Michigan Journal of Law Reform 13 (Winter 1980), pp. 231-301.

19. Lantham, Job Evaluation, pp. 30, 38.

20. Ibid., pp 2-3.

21. Ibid., p. 12.

22. Treiman, Job Evaluation.

23. L. Eyde, "Evaluating Job Evaluation," Public Personnel Management 12 (Winter 1983).

24. See text of substantive provision of Equal Remuneration Convention, 1951 (No. 100) and Recommendation, 1951 (No. 90) in ILO: Report VII (Part II) International Labour Conference, 34th Session (Geneva, 1951); Article 119 of the Treaty of Rome, 1957 establishing the European Common Community, Treaties Establishing the European Communities, Office for Official Publications of the European Communities (Luxembourg, 1973); International Labour Organization, "Equal Remuneration: Report III" (Part 4B) (Geneva, 1975).

25. J. Bellace, "A Foreign Perspective," in Comparable Worth: Issues and Alternatives, ed. E.R. Livernash (Washington, 1980), pp. 137-72, contends that "equal value" had no meaning other than equal pay for equal work in 1951. However, Convention Recommendation 90, adopted in 1951, specifically recommended the establishment of methods of objective appraisal of the work to be performed, whether by job analysis or by other procedures, with a view to providing a classification of jobs without regard to sex (Article 5).

26. J. Grune and N. Reder, "Pay Equity, An Innovative Public Policy Approach to Eliminating Sex-Based Wage Discrimination," Public Personnel Management 12 (Winter 1983), pp. 395-403, 405-7.

27. N. Reichenburg, "Labor Relations, Additional Comparable Worth Legislation Introduced," News (International Personnel Manager's Association), March 1984, pp. 6-7.

28. E. Johansen, "Managing the Revolution," Review of Public Personnel Administration 4 (Spring 1984).

29. Treiman, Job Evaluation, pp. 30-48.

30. R. Farnquist et al., "Pandora's Worth: The San Jose Experience," Public Personnel Management 12 (Winter 1983), p. 360.

31. For a discussion of the contingencies that enter

constructing such a relationship, see A. Bellack, M. Bates, and D. Glasner, "Job Evaluation: Its Role in the Comparable Worth Debate," Public Personnel Management 12 (Winter 1983), pp. 418-19.

32. H. Risher and M. Cameron, "Pay Decisions: Testing for Discrimination," Employee Relations Law Journal 7 (Winter 1981-82), p. 424.

33. Bellack et al., "Job Evaluation," pp. 418-24.

34. For an excellent history of the diffusion of civil service reform, see J. J. Couturier and R. Schick, "The Second Century of Civil Service Reform," in Public Personnel Administration, ed. S. Hays and R.C. Kearney (Englewood Cliffs, NJ, 1983), pp. 311-29; and a survey of activities of the several states, D.L. Dresang, "Diffusion of Civil Service Reform: State and Federal Government," Review of Public Personnel Administration 2 (Spring 1982), pp. 35-48.

35. Dresang, "Diffusion of Civil Service Reform," p. 44.

36. M.M. Lepper, "Affirmative Action: A Tool for Effective Personnel Management," in Public Personnel Administration, ed. S. Hays and R.C. Kearney (Englewood Cliffs, NJ, 1983), uses the term "merit" to mean "the selection of individuals based on their competence and achievement." She defines the merit system as a "network of civil service laws, rules, and regulations that jointly embrace the merit principle and is used interchangeably with 'civil service system'" (p. 239).

37. Civil Service Reform Act of 1978, P.L. 95-454, 92 Stat. 1111 (1978) (Codified at 5 USCA 2301) (b) (3) (West Supp. 1979).

38. See testimony of Alan K. Campbell, chairman, U.S. Civil Service Commission, before the Committee on Post Office and Civil Service, U.S. House of Representatives (March 14, 1979).

39 Ibid.

40. See discussion and bibliography in J. West, "Merit, Bilateralism, Equity, and Reform," Journal of Public and International Affairs 3 (Fall-Winter 1982), pp. 63-77. The discussion of merit and bilateralism draws on West's excellent analysis.

41. Ibid.

42. Ibid.

43. G.T. Sulzner, "Politics, Labor Relations, and Public Personnel Managment," Policy Studies Journal 11 (December 1982), pp. 279-89.

44. County of Washington v. Gunther, 452 U.S.161 (1981), II, 16-18, General Accounting Office. "The EEOC Has Made Limited Progress in Eliminating Employment Discrimination," September 18, 1976. See analysis in M. Tucker, Reorganization of the EEOC (Cambridge, 1978), pp. 1-10.

45. 78 Stat. 253; 42 U.S.C 2000e.

46. 86 Stat. 103; 42 U.S.C. 2000e.

47. EEOC, "Senate Confirms Eleanor Holmes Norton," 15 (1977), pp. 3-10.

48. Excerpted from a homily Commissioner Norton wrote in memory of Fannie Lou Hamer, founder of the Mississippi Freedom Democratic Party, in EEOC, "The Women Who Changed the South," Vol. 5, No. 6 (1977), p. 15.

49. R. Blumrosen, "Wage Discrimination, Sex Segregation and Title VII."

50. EEOC, "The EEOC--It Is 'A Changing,'" Vol. 6, No. 1 (1978), p. 5.

51. Federal Register, "Job Segregation and Wage Discrimination Under Title VII and the Equal Pay Act", Public Informational Hearing, November 2, 1979.

52. For a discussion of the Washington State methodology see N.D. Willis, State of Washington Comparable Worth Study (Washington, 1974, 1976); Also Treiman, Job Evaluation, pp. 97-108 and H. Remick, "An Update on Washington State," Public Personnel Management 12 (Winter 1983), pp. 390-94.

53. See Gunther v. County of Washington 452 US 161 (1981).

54. American Society for Personnel Administration and the American Compensation Association, Elements of Sound Base Pay Administration, p. 29.

55. Ibid., pp. 25-28.

56. W.F. Kay and M.C. Stevens, "Potential Impact of Concept of Comparable Worth on Public Sector Bargaining," National Public Employment Reporter 4 (March 1982), pp. 25-36.

57. J.R. Gusfield, ed., Protest, Reform and Revolt: A Reader in Social Movements, (New York, 1970), pp. vii-ix, 1-4.

58. J. Freeman, "Resource Mobilization and Strategy: A Model for Analyzing Social Movement Organization Actions," in The Dynamics of Social Movements, ed. M. Zald and J.D. McCarthy (Cambridge, MA, 1979), pp. 174-75.

59. Ibid., p. 176.

2
Who Is Seeking Change?

POLICY ACTORS AND SOCIAL MOVEMENTS

The pay equity movement is essentially rooted in the
coalitional politics of the middle and upper classes of
U.S. society, and is well within the mainstream of the
reemergent feminist movement of the 1960s.[1] Sophisticated
in using organizational resources, and in building and
maintaining issue networks, its reformist leaders direct
their efforts toward change within existing political
systems.

Several factors have shaped the pay equity movement
and are still giving it its distinct character. These
include (1) its place within the historical feminist
movement, a source of precedents; (2) the organizations
within government that arose to institutionalize protest
over the status of women, from which it draws legitimacy;
(3) the struggle of union feminists with unions' institutional bias and the place of those women in the movement
leadership; and (4) the support of women's studies centers and philanthropic institutions. The dynamic character of the pay equity movement is exampled in how the
ideas of change were taken up by organization after
organization within the post-1960s "new feminist movement," which is made up of mass-based feminist organizations, specialized litigation and research organizations,
single-issue groups, and traditional women's groups.[2]

This chapter presents the history and focus of the
early (1830-48), middle (1919-60s), and later
(post-1960s) feminist movements so as to place in a con-
tinuum the development of an integrated diffusion network
for pay equity in the late 1970s; and then delineates the
importance for social change of "insiders" and "outsiders"--feminists within government and outside it.

27

28

THE FEMINIST MOVEMENT IN HISTORICAL CONTEXT

The ideas of the early feminists in the 1830s about transforming society to alter radically women's place in it set them against the current.[3] They sought a legal standing for women to gain independence in business, and equal access to education, and the trades and professions but won no measure of acceptance or legitimacy in the politics of their time.

Seventy years intervened between the Seneca Falls Conference of the early feminists in 1848 and President Woodrow Wilson's endorsement of suffrage in 1919. A more quiescent feminism had arisen in the interim to represent women's political views. The early feminists had taken radical stances concerning the inherent equality of men and women that was everywhere denied; the later feminists seemed untroubled by it. The radical feminists had assaulted women's place; the social feminists exalted it. Radical feminism had failed to capture a mass following. The later women's movement took a different route, exploiting notions that the nation needed women's moral sensitivity and maternal virtues. The broad goal of seeking equality was replaced by the narrower goal of enfranchisement, a goal more likely to be reached in the reformist fervor of the times.

The suffragists carefully nurtured the curative ethos of traditional feminine "virtues" as they built coalitions among reform constituencies. Their campaign was masterfully planned: it created momentum for a constitutional amendment in the states while simultaneously cultivating assent by the president and congressional delegations. The leaders of the suffrage movement at the turn of the century maintained a profile of respectability, and "pursued the fight for the vote within the context of conventional ideas of woman's place."[4]

The irony was that gaining the vote only exacerbated women's problems: women had promised to bring forth reforms if enfranchised, and had given up the goals of institutional reform that would have allowed them the advantages to do so. Leaders and followers alike could not use the vote to change the social structure that assigned them to the domestic sphere of life. They lacked the "opportunity to develop a collective self-conscious" from which to act in their own political self-interest as a group.[5] When their reforms did not materialize, the social feminists of the 1920s were discredited, and the movement deteriorated. By the middle of the 1920s it had lost standing among political leaders.[6]

For almost fifty years following acceptance of the Nineteenth Amendment in 1919, women voted and worked within the narrow span of social, political, and economic roles that were essentially segregated by sex. The inequality rooted in social structure, in the allocation of different spheres of activities and roles for men and women, maintained the imbalance of power between the sexes. The vote did not address the institutionalized dependence that the early feminists had campaigned against, nor did gaining suffrage alter the social and economic valuation of women's work.

Women had always worked. Colonial women reportedly held a broad array of nontraditional occupations, such as millers, carpenters, lawyers, and owners of businesses, as well as traditional jobs.[7] By the 1830s--the time of the early feminists--the range of opportunity had narrowed appreciably, and a century later, although 10.75 million women were employed, subtle changes had further constrained job variety, continuity, pay, and status. Women's distribution among the occupations in 1930 was heavily weighted toward the menial and unskilled work.[8] Of the 1.5 million women professionals three-quarters were schoolteachers and nurses. One-tenth of all unemployed women were heads of families.[9] Despite stark evidence of the economic inequality of women from 1920 to 1970, the public's perception of the situation was remarkably at odds with the reality.[10] No matter how many women were in the labor market, their relative status there remained unchanged: their jobs were frequently segregated according to sex; they were paid less as a group than men; they had little chance for advancement.[11]

The establishment of the U.S. Women's Bureau in 1920 signaled recognition of women in the work force and electorate. But a half-century of facts, exhortation, and interest-group pressure failed to bring about much improvement for employed women. Year after year, the bureau produced voluminous, scarcely noticed statistics that were rarely acted upon. Its reports became highly stylized over the decades, repeatedly covering the same issues: the narrow band of women's occupations; the intermittence of their employment; women's necessity for incomes; dual employment as wives and mothers and wage earners; unemployment; differentials in compensation; and the effect of labor legislation on their welfare. It exemplified the limitations of government agencies having influence but no power, yet some of its accomplishments were noteworthy--it documented hazardous conditions or exploitative practices, and created national and international opportunities for exchange of ideas and interaction among traditional women's groups and trade organizations.

The bureau was a carryover from the Progressive era with its reformist zeal and scientific management techniques. It had no enforcement functions and thus its dilemma--how to sponsor reform from within government when lacking a cohesive constituency, sanctions, or incentives--had no solution. Director Mary Anderson (1920-44) failed to convince several generations of politicians of the inequities in the working environment of women. Uneducated and accustomed to union politics--Chicago style--she lacked the social skills and experience to alter the powerlessness of the agency. Where Carrie Chapman Catt had built a superb mass-based organization for the passage of suffrage, Anderson had to settle for keeping the bureau intact.

Sealander reports that "while the Bureau did not trivialize the economic problems faced by women workers...as an 'insider' it did not advocate structural changes."[12] It was as though the bureau was held captive by the traditional view of women in society and thereby "contributed to the problem even as /it/ sought a solution."[13]

Women had no political identity that commanded respect during this period. In 1920 just thirty-seven women held seats in state legislatures; women constituted only 2.7 percent of the Republican party delegates and 7.3 percent of the Democratic party delegates to the national conventions.[14] By 1925 only three women were serving in Congress; their number increased to eight in 1931 and to eleven in 1945, where it remained until the 1960s. Esther Peterson, who was appointed director of the Women's Bureau in 1961, describes a lonely landscape for women officials singled out for political recognition in that half-century. She reviews the appointment of women to high federal office from the time of suffrage to the 1960s:

> Before women obtained the right to vote, only one woman held appointive position in government--Julia Lathrop, the Head of the Children's Bureau, named to her post by President William Howard Taft in 1912. After women became voters, each succeeding president strove to convince the members of the new electorate of his concern for their welfare by naming women to positions in government. Altogether they numbered a mere handful. In 1933, President Franklin D. Roosevelt named Frances Perkins as secretary of labor. She became the first woman to hold a Cabinet post. A full twenty years passed

before the second female Cabinet member
followed--Oveta Culp Hobby, chosen by
President Dwight Eisenhower to head the
new Department of Health, Education, and
Welfare. Yet another twenty years went by
before a third woman, Carla Hills, became
secretary of Housing and Urban
Development, appointed by President Gerald
Ford.[15]

Without face or voice or model of accomplishment in
national politics, women remained unrepresented through
two world wars, even as their ranks in the work force
reached twenty million.[16] They had twice been readily
accepted in the wartime work force, but equal
compensation and opportunities were neither automatic nor
commonplace. Despite momentary War Labor Board rulings
supporting equal pay for comparable jobs held by women
producing the same quality and quantity of work as men,
the postwar wage rates perpetuated inequality.[17]

The bureau's attention to equal pay showed its two
strengths: persistence, and arranging for interest groups
to exchange views about social and economic conditions of
employed women. Equal pay appeared on the state level in
1919 in Michigan and Montana, coincident with its
incorporation in the constitution of the International
Labour Organization of the League of Nations. Nine
states had adopted it by 1937.[18] That year five national
women's organizations cooperated with the bureau to
produce reports for the International Labour Organization
on women's economic situation. By 1948 the number of
national women's civic, professional, and labor groups
participating in bureau conferences had risen to over
ninety.[19]

The 79th Congress wrestled in 1945 with an equal pay
bill that introduced the concept of comparable worth, and
stated that pay differentials based on sex constituted an
unfair labor practice. It prohibited any wage
differential for "work of a comparable character, the
performance of which requires comparable skills."[20] The
measure failed of passage then and in every subsequent
session of Congress for eighteen years.

In 1952 the Women's Bureau was more assertive. It
encouraged the establishment of a nongovernmental
lobbying organization, the National Committee for Equal
Pay, a coalition of twenty large national organizations,
to press for passage of an equal pay act.[21]

The bureau was not without flaws or critics.
Closely aligned with labor organizations, it persisted in
championing state protective laws long after objections
had been raised as to their role in limiting the
participation of women in the work force.[22] It remained
tied to a model of institutional probity, "a product of
circumstances it did not challenge and could not change
because it was already part of the structure."[23]

REAWAKENING OF PURPOSE: THE
SECOND FEMINIST REVOLUTION

The 1960s was a decade of political confrontation
over values and institutions, of protest and
preoccupation with injustice, prejudice, and presumption.
The energy with which ideas drove events and vice versa
was remarkable. After almost forty years of political
quiescence and anonymity, women found voice and cause.
The issues feminists raised set in motion political
forces that would splinter party, home, and workplace for
generations.

The changes were initially sought by social and
political elites. They began quietly, inconspicuously,
and--consistent with the careful, measured research and
coalition-based style of the Women's Bureau--as a
national commission to study the status of women. The
difference this time was the special access of new
Women's Bureau Director Esther Peterson to President
Kennedy. The bureau had wanted a national commission
since the late 1940s, and the time was now right for it.
Peterson took up the task of staff planning,
coordination, and support to develop the 1961 executive
order creating the President's Commission on the Status
of Women (PCSW). The PCSW and the state commissions that
followed are generally credited with creating the
conditions that marked the resurgence of the new feminist
movement.[24]

Representation and participation on the PCSW was
critical. Eleanor Roosevelt was appointed as chair,
Peterson vice chair. Its twenty-six members included
representatives of "both houses of Congress, the
secretaries of Labor, Commerce, and Health, Education,
and Welfare (HEW), the attorney general, the chairman of
the (then) Civil Service Commission, as well as prominent
representatives of industry, labor, education, and
women's organizations."[25] The crucial factor in its
success was that members became involved and participated
personally rather than sending representatives. The
commission also had the visible support of the president,
who attended its first meeting, and the attorney general,
who was disposed to direct action, and who issued

directive AG 1834, forbidding selecti[...]
federal service.

The PCSW's report, American Woman, [...]
work of seven subcommittees on educatio[...]
life, private employment, federal empl[...]
labor legislation, social insurance an[...]
and political rights. All documen[...]
women had been denied opportunities an[...]
men.[26] The final report, delivered [...]
October 1963, was called "Invitation to Action."

The effect of study and deliberation at the federal
and state levels of government was threefold: "(1) /It/
brought together many knowledgeable, politically active
women who otherwise would not have worked together around
matters of direct concern to women; (2). . . unearthed
ample evidence of women's unequal status. . .; and (3). .
. /created/ a climate of expectations that something
would be done."[27]

The legislative action that followed was only the
beginning of a profound reorientation in politics,
administration, and the law of the views of and about
women and their activities. Eleanor Roosevelt and other
PCSW members testified for the Equal Pay Act considered
in 1963. By that time, twenty-two states had adopted
similar legislation.[28] The reference to equal pay for
work of comparable value had been removed to expedite
passage of the act in Congress, but after a
seventeen-year battle, partisans were satisfied with a
partial victory.[29]

Legislative reform led to an enormous surge of
measures affecting every dimension of civil and political
life. Carson identifies four kinds of reform considered:
individual, meaning self-inspection and renewal;
institutional, meaning directed toward changing
organizational behavior; liberal, in the sense of
removing legal restriction to enhance individual liberty;
and ameliorative, meaning to use the power of government
to improve conditions of human life.[30] The widespread
expectation of improvement was rooted within the
pragmatism of the twentieth-century mind; utopian goals
were set aside for plans tailored to fragmented political
institutions.[31]

WOMEN IN POLITICS: THE RISE OF THE PRAGMATISTS

The legislative and executive activity of the PCSW
was directed toward remedying problems outlined in its
findings. The Equal Pay Act of 1963 (EPA), the Civil
Rights Act of 1964 (Title VII), and Executive Order 11246

...65 as amended in 1967 by Executive Order 11375 ...arding nondiscrimination by federal contractors) ...mpled both the work of the PCSW and the adroitness of ...men members of Congress and other advocates to follow through on opportunities within the institutions where they had access.[32] Women were not widely represented in elective office in the 1960s, and their attention was concentrated more on local and state concerns and politics.[33] Surveys of women state legislators found them little sympathetic toward the notions that women as a class had been discriminated against.[34] Disagreements among women themselves over issues of fact and value concerning women's status, rights, and responsibilities would go on for decades.

The women's movement did not exist at the time of the Equal Pay Act or introduction of the Civil Rights Act of 1964, but emerged soon after. It was not until 1969 and the establishment of the President's Task Force on Women's Rights and Responsibilities that the term "women's rights" was used in government. By then the two major women's rights organizations--the National Organization for Women (NOW) and Women's Equity Action League (WEAL) had been established.[35] NOW had been organized in 1966 by Betty Friedan and twenty-eight women who were attending the Third National Conference of Commissions on the Status of Women. As delegates, they had become frustrated when the conference failed to ratify a resolution urging that the Equal Employment Opportunity Commission treat sex discrimination with the same seriousness as race discrimination. Ten days before the conference, Representative Martha Griffiths had delivered a sharp rebuke in the House directed at EEOC commissioners and staff,[36] who, it was alleged, had derided the notion of enforcing the sex discrimination provisions of the Civil Rights Act. Friedan thought Griffiths's stand merited strong support, the majority of delegates demurred, and NOW was formed in reaction.

NOW was created to influence national legislation, and to build a mass-based national organization. It drew on the experience and training of its members in party politics, government, and the civil rights movement to practice what its founders knew best: media engagement to gain leverage for pressuring government action. Staged media events-- picket lines and protests-- complemented lobbying.[37] NOW's headquarters were in Chicago, and it opened an office in Washington at the beginning of the 93d Congress. At NOW's 1967 national conference in Washington, it adopted a "bill of rights" calling for "passage of the ERA, enforcement of employment rights laws, establishment of child care centers, as well as equal education and acknowledgement of the 'right of women to control their reproductive lives.'"38

The immediate effect of the 1967 resolution was loss of the support of more moderate women professionals, who disassociated themselves from NOW's sweeping social doctrines and formed the Women's Equity Action League in 1968 as an alternative. WEAL adopted plans to intervene in political systems through lobbying and litigation unimpeded by NOW's more radical image. Its members believed that abortion was too divisive an issue, Friedan too controversial, and NOW's mission too diffuse to command the respect of lawmakers.39 WEAL concentrated its efforts on the state and local levels, establishing chapters in forty states by 1971. In 1972 it incorporated its Education and Legal Defense Fund (WLDF), as had NOW somewhat earlier (NOW-LDEF). WEAL filed complaints on behalf of women faculty members regarding noncompliance with Executive Order 11246 against more than three hundred colleges and universities.

A secondary effect of NOW's resolution was that some of its provisions received sustained and serious legislative attention. The National Women's Party (NWP), founded in 1916, had lobbied Congress from 1923 to 1972 for an Equal Rights Amendment (ERA). NOW's endorsement lent the issue salience. In January 1970, Senator Birch Bayh announced that the Senate Judiciary Subcommittee on Constitutional Amendments would hold hearings on the Equal Rights Amendment.

Passage of the ERA in 1972 made NOW's directors realize that NOW's national structure was not comprehensive enough to affect grass roots politics; a "mid-level" of state organizations to seek ratification was needed.40 Similarly, WEAL and the National Women's Political Caucus (NWPC) examined their structures and subsequently opened Washington offices. The three organizations formed the Women's Lobby in 1972 to work with political action groups to coordinate "passage of bills in Congress for the benefit of women."41 The Women's Lobby was only the first formalization of fluid coalitions of mass-based, single-issue, and specialized research and litigation groups that had worked on women's rights issues in the 1960s and would increase in the 1970s and 1980s. The predominant factor contributing to the success of the coalitions was their knowledge of political and administrative systems, and ability to tailor their lobbying efforts accordingly. They were also fortunate in that women's rights issues could be disaggregated such that a defeat in one area did not spill over to discredit another.42 Part of the benefit of coalitional politics was the favorable image created among congressmen and staffs of "a serious constituent interest in women's rights."[43]

There was much for women's rights lobbyists in
Washington to celebrate in 1972. Congress considered and
passed more women's rights legislation in that year than
it had in the entire preceding century; in addition to
the ERA and Title IX it put on the books the Equal
Employment Opportunity ACT of 1972, which extended the
coverage of Title VII to state and local governments, and
the State and Local Fiscal Act of 1972, as amended, which
mandated that jurisdictions receiving revenue sharing
funds not discriminate in employment on the basis of
sex.[44] That year, too, the state of Washington began
considering a job evaluation study, the first in a decade
of its studies.

The Equal Pay Act and Title VII had been tightened
to seal off loopholes, and Title IV of the Civil Rights
Act was amended to give school districts funds to combat
sex discrimination.[45] The speed with which change had
occurred was phenomenal. Millsap recounts a
congressional aide's amazement: "We put sex
discrimination provisions into everything. There was no
opposition."[46] Gelb and Klein speculate that the response
was possible "in part because of the existing body of
race-related legislation."[47]

The year was critically important to comparable
worth because of the extension in coverage of Title VII
to state and local government, and also because of the
policy shift of the EEOC away from the doctrine of
individual intent in discrimination. EEOC's guidelines
for 1972 appear to follow the broader interpretation of
discrimination established by the Supreme Court in Griggs
v. Duke Power Company,[48] stating, in part:

> The most pervasive discriminatory
> practices now are recognized to result
> from seemingly neutral policies and
> practices within basic employment systems.
> However neutral they appear, however
> neutral and benign in intent, these
> systems produce highly discriminatory
> effects; neutral practices also perpetuate
> discriminatory effects of past
> discriminatory practices.[59]

INSTITUTIONALIZING PROTEST

A significant factor in the success of the women's
rights lobby in the 1970s that would be decisive in the
development of comparable worth as well was the

ever-widening network of sympathizers in government and
the media who could move information critical to
decisions. There were now any number of women
professionals--insiders in government--who had time,
information, or expertise to contribute to the initiation
and implementation of policy issues.

Commissions for Women

Since the late 1960s one of the more effective
institutions to provide continuity in keeping
policymakers and interest groups informed on women's
issues has been commissions for women. Initially, a great
deal of direction came from Women's Bureau personnel who
helped found and staff two liaison agencies with the
state commissions: the Interdepartmental Committee on the
Status of Women (ICSW) and the Citizens Advisory Council
on the Status of Women (CACSW).[50] CACSW produced studies
and policy memoranda for implementing the Civil Rights
Act of 1964, and pressed for uniformity in state laws
regarding women's civil and economic rights. Early
participants in the President's Commission on the Status
of Women (PCSW) thought that the commission had made
discussions of women's roles and status respectable,
although its recommendations were "temperate,"[51] its
style incremental. Most analysts place the PCSW before
the women's rights movement and not as part of it; the
state commissions are usually credited with playing more
than just a symbolic and legitimizing role.

The commissions were both cooptable and cooptive in
the development of policy and constituencies of change.
The PCSW, the state commissions, and feminists within the
EEOC became a potentially cooptable sector of the women's
movement as the first women's group in government. They
were exposed to the facts of women's status, and had
firsthand knowledge of the sex discrimination cases.[52]
They shared similar experiences and perspectives, they
were "receptive to the particular new ideas of the
incipient movement...not faced with structural or
ideological barriers to action,"[53] and they were expected
to be advocates and agents for improving the status of
women. Their strength lay in functioning as an
information network and testifying on behalf of
legislation for women.

The U.S. Citizens' Advisory Council on the Status of
Women and the state commissions played a cooptive role in
sponsoring conferences, publications, research, and
legislative reference services regarding state and
federal laws and private economic activities pertinent to
the welfare of women. They developed links among

specialized groups and individuals, and legitimized coalitions seeking policy changes. On the issue of comparable worth they became a substantial element in the diffusion network of "insiders" in government who kept one another current on its progress in the states and, in some cases, wrote legislation and worked to insure implementation.[54]

In 1980 there were forty-three active state commissions, including those of the District of Columbia and Puerto Rico: eleven were either incorporated into government agencies, or were independent commissions; eighteen were accountable to the office of the governor; and the remainder reported to such entities as departments of human resources or labor, or to the legislature. There are also regional and local commissions. In many instances where state commissions were abolished or "in exile," local commissions remained active.[55]

State and local commissions represent a wide spectrum of opinion on role-change issues, of course-- especially regarding abortion and the ERA. More than half reported in 1980 that their need for funding made them vulnerable to pressure. A number of commissions facing "abolition or an 'unhealthy' environment, have established alternative commissions outside the government."[56] This includes the commission in the state of Washington.

Of the thirty-three states with some form of comparable worth activity, eleven have commissions on the status of women, each of whose annual budget is in excess of $100,000, necessitating professional staff. Most often commissions are not dominated by boards but are professionalized and look to staff to select issues and give continuity in policy. Commissions and their staffs have provided two critical functions in comparable worth's development: serving as an information clearinghouse and legitimizing coalitions.[57]

Community values have a material effect on the political context in which the various commissions function, and in turn on the commissions' activism or conservatism. Some are models of pluralist politics, legitimizing issues and facilitating policies; others rely on protest activities if they feel it is appropriate; still others follow a bureaucratic model, bargaining and negotiating with agencies, interests, and constituency groups;[58] and some are comfortable with symbolic roles and issues. The expression of feminism in policy depends upon the political and cultural environment of which the commissions are a product.

WOMEN AT WORK

The role of women unionists who have emerged from
struggles with institutional bias in their own
organizations to become leaders in the pay equity
movement has been less variable than that of the
commissions. Their involvement has meant a range of
strategies and tactics not usually found in
interest-group politics. The PCSW report of 1961,
American Woman, and the passage of the EPA in 1963 and
Title VII in 1964 attracted the attention of women
opinion leaders everywhere, and especially those in trade
unions.

The prohibitions against discrimination on the basis
of sex found in Title VII of the Civil Rights Act of 1964
applied to unions as well as employers. "Prior to 1964,
the duty of fair representation did not require the
admission into unions of minorities, or women, even
though the union had the exclusive authority to bargain
for them."[59] After that women could no longer be denied
membership, and their strategic importance to unions grew
over the late 1960s and early 1970s as shifts occurred in
power relations between the older industrial unions,
which were losing members, and the reform-minded unions,
which were gaining them.[60] The latter were aggressive in
forming political action committees to influence
political parties, and were increasingly sensitive to
demands of minorities and women within their ranks.
While private sector unions grew by only 3.7 percent
between 1968 and 1974, public-sector unions at the state
and local levels grew by 58.9 percent.[61]

Union Policies Toward Working Women

Although it was not apparent in the late 1960s
whether or how changes might occur in the internal
allocation of power and roles within unions, union
interpretations of labor laws concerning women began to
be scrutinized by women unionists. In particular, some
concluded that Title VII superseded state protective laws
that unions had supported for decades. Litigation
following enactment of the EPA and Title VII revealed
"the ambiguity in American industry of sex
discrimination.../that/ originated in and was intertwined
with laws which purported to protect women."[62]
Protective legislation had become enshrined in 1908 in
Muller v. Oregon. The Supreme Court sustained a ruling
concerning an Oregon law that restricted the number of
hours women could work, basing its decision on the
"inherent differences between the sexes," and women's
"different (i.e., maternal) functions in life."[63]

In the fifty-odd years between Muller and the Civil Rights Act of 1964, several developments had eroded the basis of the judicial emphasis on a woman's family role as the determinant of her legal existence. First, women were working in greater numbers: in 1900, 5.1 million; in 1970, 34.5 million.[64] Women as individuals and groups could no longer be relegated to the domestic sphere. Second, "once the courts were confronted with a statutory commitment to sexual equality, they could not avoid perceiving the connection between protection and restriction."[65] Although some of the protective laws were an outgrowth of concern for unsafe, unsanitary, and exploitive working conditions, such legislation also had strong support during its origination amongst "organized labor which saw women workers as competitors to men."[66]

Polling of more than forty national unions in 1967 found that much of labor wanted to retain protective legislation. This is not surprising, considering the unrepresentativeness of union leadership: in 1972, 142 of 177 trade unions had no women officials;[67] and from 1950 to 1970, there had been only two women presidents of national unions.[68] One break in the half-century of support by unions for protective legislation came from women members of the United Auto Workers (UAW) in California who sought NOW's help in persuading the UAW Women's Department to take a stand against protective legislation--which the department later did. In 1967 the UAW was the first large union to speak out to tighten the application of Bona Fide Occupational Qualifications (BFOQ). The action showed foresight. In 1960, of the twenty-four million employed women, only three and a half million belonged to unions; in 1973, of the thirty-four million, only four million.[69] Women were a vast labor pool for potential recruitment, particularly those in the public sector and industries with a disproportionate number of female blue-collar and clerical workers.

Women in Unions: Coalition of Labor Union Women

The UAW action in 1967 initiated a chain of events that inverted the position of the unions regarding protective legislation.[70] Next came an intensive promotion among all women union members to build up a momentum for equal rights and opportunities for women within the unions themselves.[71]

Although many groups were formed in the early 1970s to articulate women's concerns within unions, a coterie emerged in 1974 with the skills to build a nationwide organization, the Coalition of Labor Union Women (CLUW). Their planning meeting in June 1973 in Chicago attracted

two hundred women and was followed by regional hearings
throughout 1973. In March 1974 more than three thousand
union women from fifty-eight international unions met in
Chicago. CLUW's founders outmaneuvered the more radical
women, who wanted the organization to take stands on
support for United Farm Workers and other controversial
issues,[72] guiding the assembly to adopt a statement of
purpose that constrained the CLUW to the programmatic
issues of organizing women, bringing affirmative action
to the workplace, and seeking change through political
action and legislation.[73] Additionally, it would seek
publicity, visibility, and coalitions to make union women
a force within the women's movement, and within the
national and local union structure.

High on the CLUW list of situations to remedy were
the powerlessness of women within unions and the status
of women in the workplace. At the fourth national
conference, in 1979, resolutions favoring "equal pay for
equal value" or comparable worth and increased female
representation on the executive boards of unions were
approved.[74] These were logical extensions of the views
of the predominant contingent within CLUW, the
public-sector members. Of CLUW's membership of six
thousand in 1979, more than 60 percent were government
and white-collar workers in thirty chapters nationwide.[75]
Another one of CLUW's major accomplishments was to "bring
together the general counsels of 16 international unions
to discuss comparable worth strategies."[76]

Much happened nationally between 1973, the first
CLUW meeting, and 1979. The job evaluation study in the
State of Washington had gone through two stages and was
embarking on a third.[77] The International Labour
Organization had passed another resolution in 1975
reaffirming its support for adoption of the concept of
comparable worth by its member nations. Canada passed
legislation in 1977 "to eliminate job ghettos and push
for a reappraisal of existing compensation and job
evaluation systems in organizations under federal
jurisdictions,"[79] and had set up administrative
machinery to implement this. Several state job
evaluation studies in the United States were modeled
after the Washington study. Many of the elements for
social action were in place. What remained was the
development of an integrated diffusion network.[80]

Working women's issues were a topic of NOW's tenth
national convention. Its package of concrete goals had
been generated by its Labor Task Force and was approved
by the delegates, a victory for a coordinated effort of
labor union women and NOW. The goals included "full
support for union organizing and for the overturning of

the Bennett Amendment, which /had made/ it impossible to
sue under Title VII of the Civil Rights Act for 'equal
pay for work of comparable value.'"[81]

Women trade unionists had fought successfully to
put comparable worth onto the agenda of numerous groups.
At the 1975 International Women's Year Conference in
Mexico City Joan Goodin was the international liaison for
CLUW, representing trade union women. Her mission was
"to incorporate union women's concerns into the official
U.S. position...." She recalls "the battle she had in
Mexico City" when the Russian delegation refused to
accept a proposed U.S. amendment to the World Plan of
Action for the UN Decade of Women that would change the
phrase "equal pay for equal work" to "equal pay for work
of equal value."[82] The amendment did pass, and the next
task was to create a broader base of support for it in
the United States. An attentive public existed among
women's groups--attorneys, legislators, professional
women, and administrators. They had only to be
activated.

SYNTHESIS: THE BEGINNING OF AN
INTEGRATED DIFFUSION NETWORK

The PCSW 1961 report had initiated a far-reaching
examination of the status of women in the United States.
The reverberations in the form of burgeoning advocacy
groups inside and outside government helped make social
legislation on the national and state levels a reality.
But the resources of traditional women's groups and NOW
had been hard pressed by expensive political excursions,
such as the ratification process of the ERA, which had
ended in defeat.[83] The state commissions on the status
of women had more stability in funding; they were able to
continue their invaluable network activities during the
ratification period and still emerge as coordinators with
a legitimizing influence on feminist policy issues.
Nationally, "under the Carter Administration, there were
now finally enough women inside to make a difference."[84]
Several needs came to the fore in the 1970s: formal
research on women to assist in passing legislation;
professional legal counsel to complement voluntary
lobbying; and money to fund policy research centers and
seminars to plan integrated strategies.

Early in the decade, Irene Tinker and women of
Organizations for Professional Women met with Barbara
Newell, the new president of Wellesley College, and
established the Center for Research on Women in Higher
Education and the Professions.[85] In May 1975, the
center's Conference on Occupational Segregation brought

together an impressive group of individuals who would
shape the dialogue on comparable worth for the next
decade, among them Heidi Hartmann, who, with Donald
Treiman, would edit the EEOC-commissioned National
Academy of Sciences report Women, Work and Wages, and
Winn Newman, then counsel to the International Union of
Electrical Workers,[86] who later became counsel for AFSCME
and successfully pursued two federal district court
rulings on comparable worth. Research centers were
established at a steady pace over the intervening years.
The National Council for Research on Women now serves as
an "umbrella group for 21 existing centers nationwide."[87]

Responsible, often professionally trained elites
were now in place to carry forward the intensive
research, lobbying, and litigation necessary to bring
role equity policy issues to life in fact.[88] Money came
in large part from private philanthropic foundations,
which sponsored much of the work of women's policy
centers and underwrote various women's rights and legal
defense funds.[89]

In late 1978, Winn Newman interested two women
associated with the Antioch School of Law in featuring
comparable worth as a conference topic. They thus began
"The Committee on Pay Equity, a national coalition of
labor, women's, public interest, legal, government and
educational organizations,"[90] which in 1980 was renamed
the National Committee on Pay Equity (NCPE). Their
Conference on Pay Equity was held in October 1979, funded
by two major foundations, AFSCME and the Women's
Bureau.[91] The conference and the committee's Manual on
Pay Equity both served as diffusion instruments[92] for the
several hundred "experts and activists who had gathered
to share information, discuss problems, and to begin to
develop a coordinated strategy to raise women's wages."[93]
The manual integrated the legal, evaluative, policy, and
collective bargaining experiences of proponents of
comparable worth, and outlined legal, political, and
organizational moves available to activists on the
subnational level. It was the first comprehensive action
guide in four critical areas: employment statistics;
case law under Title VII and the EPA; EEOC activities,
regarding both rules and policies; and state and local
legislative policies and collective bargaining
initiatives directed toward studying job evaluation
practices and/or restructuring them to bring them into
congruence with comparable worth criteria.

The conclusions of the conference were fairly
explicit: by itself no single strategy had
worked--comparable worth had been considered but rejected
in debate over the EPA in 1963 and was unlikely to find

much support in less liberal Congresses;[94] litigation
cases and strategies had been poorly selected and had set
damaging precedents;[95] litigation under the broad Title
VII prohibitions of discrimination seemed to be stymied
by the application of the standards of the EPA under the
Bennett Amendment (Lemons v. City of Denver, 1980;
Christensen v. State of Iowa, 1977); and that comparable
worth job evaluation studies to document discrimination
in wages for women looked promising but were
informational and lacked enforcement mechanisms. The
manual was replete with examples and exhortations to
direct comparable worth to the subnational level, where
feminists had some organizational and political
advantages, and where strategies coordinated and deployed
in the public sector through "studies, organizing,
legislation, collective bargaining, lobbying and
litigation"[96] could be effective.[97]

While many of the leaders of the National Committee
for Pay Equity (NCPE) are union trained, employed, or
affiliated, their base of support appears fairly broad.[98]
The NCPE has been active in providing speakers on pay
equity at national conferences of state legislators and
of professional associations, congressional and EEOC
hearings, and individual state legislatures.[99] Overall,
the strength of the movement lies in its network quality
and grass roots support. Chapters 4 and 5 tell how the
issue has developed politically across the nation, where
changes have been tried, and with what outcomes.

NOTES

1. Much of the discussion of the pay equity
movement in this paragraph draws on examples of women in
politics presented in the work of J. Gelb and M.L.
Palley, Women and Public Policies (Princeton, 1982),
pp.3-13. The terms "new feminist movement" and "the
second feminist movement, post-1960s" refer to the social
movement that began in the early 1960s.
2. Ibid., p. 4.
3. W.H. Chafe, The American Woman (Oxford, 1972);
W.L. O'Neill, Everyone Was Brave (New York, 1969); and J.
Freeman, The Politics of Women's Liberation (New York,
1975) provide excellent overviews of the successive
stages of the women's movement.
4. Chafe, The American Woman, p. 13.
5. Ibid., p. 46.
6. Ibid., p. 29.

7. J.A. Sealander, "The Women's Bureau, 1920-1950: Federal Reaction to Wage Earnings" (Ph.D. diss., Duke University, 1977).

8. The 1930 Census showed women distributed among the following occupational categories: 3,180,307, domestic and personal; 1,986,830, clerical; 1,886,307, manufacturing and mechanical; 1,526,234, professional; 962,680, trade; 909,939, agriculture; and 281,204, transportation and communication. See M. Pidgeon Women in the Economy (Washington, DC, 1937), p. 1.

9. Ibid.

10. Chafe, The American Woman, p. 64; and V.K. Oppenheimer, The Female Labor Force in the United States (Westport, CT, 1970), pp. 40-63.

11. E. Johansen, "Managing the Revolution: The Case of Comparable Worth," Review of Public Personnel Administration 4 (Spring 1984): 8.

12. Sealander, "The Women's Bureau," p. 7. See also M. Anderson, Women at Work (as told to Mary N. Wilson; Minneapolis, 1951).

13. Sealander, "The Women's Bureau."

14. R. Clausen, "Women and Their Organizations," in Women Organizing, ed. B. Cummings and V. Schuck (Metuchen, NJ, 1979), p. 128.

15. E. Peterson, "The Kennedy Commission," in Women in Washington, vol. 7, ed. I. Tinker (Beverly Hills, 1983), p. 2.

16. There were, of course, accomplished women who claimed national and international attention during this era, such as Eleanor Roosevelt. A distinction is made between those women who had independent national reputations in politics and those whose reputations were established originally through marital status.

17. Chafe, The American Woman, p. 155.

18. Pidgeon, Women in the Economy, p. 204.

19. Ibid., p. iv; and Women's Bureau, Women's Bureau Conference, (Washington, DC, February 1948), pp. 191-93.

20. P.S. Foner, Women and the American Labor Market, World War I to the Present (New York, 1979), p. 398.

21. M.M. Simchak, "Equal Pay in the United States," International Labor Review 103 (June 1971), p. 549.

22. For a discussion of the platform and activities of the National Women's Party regarding the Equal Rights Amendment see Chafe, The American Woman, pp. 112-32. Also J. Freeman, Women: A Feminist Perspective (New York, 1983), discusses the Supreme Court rulings concerning protective labor laws, as does J.A. Baer, The Chains of Protection (Westport, CT, 1978).

23. Sealander, "The Women's Bureau," p. ii.

24. C. East, "Newer Commissions," in Women in Washington, vol. 7, ed. I. Tinker (Beverly Hills, 1983), p. 35, reports that there were seven state commissions established during the life of the original PCSW. It was

not until 1967 that all states reportedly had
commissions. In 1980, forty-five commissions remained
operative. Women's Bureau, Commissions for Women: Moving
Into 1980 (Washington, DC, 1980).
25. Peterson, "Kennedy Commission," p. 27.
26. Ibid., p. 28.
27. Freeman, Politics of Women's Liberation, p. 52.
28. Women's Bureau, Economic Indicators Relating to
Equal Pay, No. 9 (Washington, DC, 1963).
29. 108 Congressional Record 14767-70 (1963); 109
Congressional Record 9197-98 (1963); Ibid., 8914-15
(1963); and ibid., 9761-62 (1963).
30. C.B. Carson, "The Mind of the Reformer," in
American Political Radicalism, ed. G. Abcarian (Waltham,
MA, 1971), pp. 265-77.
31. M.L. Carden, "The Experimental Utopia in
America," Daedalus, Spring 1965, p. 418.
32. An oral history recounting of the remarkable
presence of mind of Representative Martha Griffiths
during debate on the Civil Rights Act of 1964; she
pointed out that if protections were to apply to blacks,
they had to apply to women as well. In F.S. Ingersoll,
"Former Congresswomen Look Back," in Women in Washington,
vol. 7, ed. I. Tinker (Beverly Hills, 1983), pp. 196-99.
33. M.K. Jennings and R. Niemi, Generations and
Politics (Princeton, 1981).
34. J.J. Kirkpatrick, Political Woman (New York,
1974), p. 164, found that approximately 60 percent of the
women state legislators polled in her survey expressed
opposition to the women's liberation movement.
35. The National Women's Political Caucus (NWPC), a
multipartisan organization to support full participation
of women in the political process, was not formed until
1971.
36. See Representative Griffiths's speech, "Women
Are Being Deprived Legal Rights by the Equal Employment
Opportunity Commission," Congressional Record--House
13689-13694 (June 20, 1966).
37. J. Freeman, "Resource Mobilization and Strategy:
A Model Formalizing Social Movement Through Organization
Action," in The Dynamics of Social Movements, ed. M. Zald
and J.D. McCarthy (Cambridge, MA, 1979), pp. 178-79.
38. M. Rawalt, "The Equal Rights Amendment," in
Women in Washington, vol. 7, ed. I. Tinker (Beverly
Hills, 1983), pp. 47-78.
39. A. Daniels, "Feminism and Unions," in Women
Organizing, ed. B. Cummings and V. Schuck (Metuchen, NJ,
1979), pp. 133-34.
40. Freeman, "Resource Mobilization and Strategy,"
p. 184.
41. F. Carter, "Women Lobbyists Incorporate for Full
Scale Action for Women," The Woman Activist 2 (November
1972), as cited in A. Costain, "Lobbying for Equal

Credit," in Women Organizing, ed. B. Cummings and V. Schuck (Metuchen, NJ, 1979), p. 82.

42. Gelb and Palley, Women and Public Policies, p. 170.

43. Freeman, Women, p. 394.

44. J. Gelb and E. Klein, Women's Movements: Organizing for Change in the 1980s (New York, 1983), p. 42.

45. M. A. Millsap, "Sex Equity in Education," in Women in Washington, vol. 7, ed. I. Tinker (Beverly Hills, 1983), p. 94.

46. Ibid.

47. Gelb and Klein, Women's Movements, p. 42.

48. Griggs v. Duke Power Company, 401 U.S. 424 (1971).

49. The EEOC policy statement is referenced as U.S. EEOC pII-3 in J. O'Neill, "Women and the Labor Market," in House Subcommittees on Human Resources and Civil Service Compensation and Employee Benefits of the Committee on Post Office and Civil Service, Pay Equity Hearings, September 16, 21, 30 and December 2, 1982, 97th Cong., 2d sess., 1982, p. 1414.

50. East, "Newer Commissions," pp. 35-48.

51. Ibid., p. 35.

52. Freeman, Politics of Women's Liberation, p. 67.

53. Ibid., p. 68.

54. Johansen, "Managing the Revolution."

55. Local commissions include: California, 36; Florida, 14; Maryland, 12; Louisana,9; Indiana, New Jersey, and North Carolina, 6; and Texas and Virginia, 5. The commissions are usually located in the major population centers, either cities or counties.

56. Women's Bureau, Commissions for Women, p. 10.

57. Johansen, "Managing the Revolution"; and E. Johansen, "From Social Doctrine to Implementation: The Case of Comparable Worth," Policy Studies Review (Summer 1984, forthcoming).

58. D. Stewart, The Women's Movement: Community Politics in the United States (New York, 1980), pp. 113-14.

59. R. Blumrosen, "Wage Discrimination, Job Segregation, and Title VII of the Civil Rights Act of 1964," University of Michigan Journal of Law Reform 12 (Spring 1979), p. 445.

60. See R. Walters, "Reform Ripples Reaching Labor," National Journal 7 (January 1975), p. 149. Union membership in nonagricultural employment declined from .2 percent to 12.7 percent in forty-six states from 1970 to 1980. See Census Bureau, "Labor Organization Membership--Total and Percent of Nonagricultural Employment by State, 1970-1981," Statistical Abstract, 1983, p. 409.

61. N.R. Peirce, "Employment Report/Public Employee

Unions Show Rise in Membership Militancy," National Journal 7 (August 1975), pp. 1239-1249.

62. Baer, Chains of Protection, p. 216.

63. 208 U.S. 412 (1908).

64. "President's Economic Report for 1973," Weekly Compilation of Presidential Documents, (January 30), p. 101.

65. Baer, Chains of Protection, p. 216.

66. Freeman, Women, p. 384. Foner, Women and the American Labor Market, p. 360, reports that women were barred from union membership in some industries during the war because of closed shop agreements. At the UAW convention, only thirty of the two thousand delegates were women, p. 366.

67. Ibid., p. 497.

68. A. Cook, "Women and American Trade Unions," Annals of American Academy of Social and Political Science 375 (January 1968), p. 126.

69. Foner, Women and the American Labor Market, p. 505.

70. This includes a dramatic turnabout from opposition to support for the Equal Rights Amendment by both the unions and the Women's Bureau. See list of supporters in J.K. Boles, The Politics the Equal Rights Amendment (New York, 1979), pp. 196-99.

71. See Foner, Women and the American Labor Market, for description of founding of Women's Alliance to Gain Equality (WAGE), pp. 498-572; also N. Seifer and B. Wertheimer, "New Approaches to Collective Power: Four Working Women's Organizations," in Women Organizing, ed. B. Cummings and V. Schuck (Metuchen, NJ, 1979), pp. 152-208.

72. Foner, Women and the American Labor Market, p. 512; and J. Field, "The Coalition of Labor Union Women," Political Affairs 54 (March 1975), pp. 3-12.

73. J.M. Goodin, "Working Women: The Pros and Cons of Unions," in Women in Washington, vol. 7, ed. I. Tinker (Beverly Hills, 1983), p. 142.

74. J. Grune, ed., Manual on Pay Equity, (Washington, DC, 1979), p. 140.

75. Seifer and Wertheimer, "New Approaches to Collective Power," p. 160.

76. International Personnel Manager's Association (IPMA), Union Action Regarding the Comparable Worth Issue, no. 5 (1983), p. 16.

77. N.D. Willis, State of Washington Comparable Worth Study (Seattle, 1974, 1976). For list of chronology of activities in this period, see Appendix A.

78. Sec. 11, Canadian Human Rights Act.

79. Canada, Human Rights Commission, Methodology and Principles for Applying Section 11 of the Canadian Human Rights Act (Ottawa, 1983), p. 2.

80. Grune, Manual on Pay Equity p. 115.

81. Foner, *Women and the American Labor Market*, p. 489.

82. Goodin, "Working Women," p. 141.

83. For costs incurred by advocates in connection with the Equal Rights Amendment Amendment, see Boles, *Politics of the Equal Rights Amendment*, pp. 25, 63-65.

84. I. Tinker, "Women Organize for Change," in *Women in Washington*, vol. 7, ed. I. Tinker (Beverly Hills, 1983), p. 45.

85. I. Tinker, "Women Develop Strategies for Influencing Policy," in *Women in Washington*, vol. 7, ed. I. Tinker (Beverly Hills, 1983), p. 163.

86. 631 F.2d 1094 (3d Cir.); cert. denied, 449 U.S. 1009 (1980).

87. Tinker, "Women Develop Strategies for Influencing Policy," p. 163.

88. Gelb and Palley, *Women and Public Policies*, pp. 5-8.

89.Foundation contributions constituted 100 percent of the funding for American Civil Liberties Union-Women's Rights Project (ACLU-WRP); 90 percent, Center for Law and Social Policy-Women's Right Project (CLASP-WRO); 32 percent, NOW Legal Defense and Education Fund (NOW-LDEF); 19 percent, WEAL Fund; and 59 percent, Women's Legal Defense Fund (WLDF). See ibid., p. 44. The 1975 Wellesley Conference was funded by the Carnegie Corporation of New York; see M. Blaxall and B. Reagan, eds., *Women and the Workplace: The Implication of Occupational Segregation* (Chicago, 1976), p. ix.

90. Grune, *Manual on Pay Equity*, p. 3.

91. Ibid., p. 9.

92. The term "diffusion" is used in this study to refer to theories developed by Everett Rogers and others, cited by J. L. Walker, "The Diffusion of Innovations Among the Several States," *American Political Science Review* 63 (1969), pp. 880-99.

93. Grune, *Manual on Pay Equity*, p. 3.

94. D. Haener, "Letter to the Women's Bureau," in *Manual on Pay Equity*, ed. J. Grune (Washington, DC, 1979), pp. 66-67.

95. C. Wilson, "The IUE's Approach to Comparable Worth," in *Manual on Pay Equity*, ed. J. Grune (Washington, DC, 1979), pp. 89-90.

96. Grune, *Manual on Pay Equity*, p. 115.

97. Johansen, "From Social Doctrine to Implementation."

98. Nancy Pearlman, National Committee on Pay Equity (NCPE) chair in 1982, was one of the founding members of CLUW. Joy Ann Grune, NCPE executive director 1979-1984, was assistant director of the Labor and Humanities Project of AFL-CIO Labor Institute for Human Enrichment in Washington, DC. Of the nineteen groups represented on

the NCPE board, half are labor unions. The 1982 board
included institutional representatives from: Center for
Women in Government, SUNY Albany; AFSCME; Business and
Professional Women (BPW); Communication Workers of
America (CWA); National Association of Puerto Rican
Women; National Committee on Household Employment; IUE;
American Nursing Association; CLUW; League of Women
Voters (LWV); National Education Association (NEA); NOW;
9 to 5; National Association of Working Women; UAW;
Women's Right's Project-American Civil Liberties Union
(ACLU-WRP); National Urban League; Service Employees
International Union (SEIU); and Women's Legal Defense
Fund (WLDF).

99. Carole Wilson, general counsel for IUE and NCPE
board member; Nancy Pearlman, NCPE chair; Cathy Collette,
board representative for AFSCME; and Joy Ann Grune, NCPE
executive director (1980-1984), officially represented
comparable worth, and, with Winn Newman, general counsel
for AFSCME, constitute its most active spokespersons.
They have appeared as speakers at numerous professional
association meetings; EEOC hearings; congressional
hearings; and meetings of state legislators and other
officials.

3
How Changes Are Sought

THREE MODELS OF POLITICAL CHANGE:
PLURALIST, BUREAUCRATIC, AND RADICAL

The movement of comparable worth from principle to policies and from an ideology to programs has depended upon the availability of the symbolic and actual resources of its sponsors during agenda setting and implementation, and the value structure or receptivity of the policy environment. Although coalitions have tended to be the same regardless of locale--women officeholders, public-sector unions, and staffs of women's commissions--agenda-setting strategies have varied from open conflict to administrative remedies.

The agenda-setting strategies reflect the traditional use of public policies to assist the economic advancement of women through incremental tactics that focus on narrow role-equity issues to build legislative support. But the coalitions made important additions: participation by affected groups in the implementation of policies; and collective bargaining and litigation to insure administrative attention to the goals of the sponsors.

In the implementation stage, however, it appears that differences once more emerge. In some cases advocates and administrators each find the bargaining and conflict over the regulatory aspects of classification and pay to be to their partisan and mutual advantage. In other instances, less so.

This chapter constructs an analytic framework that accounts for the changing presentation and uses of comparable worth: first as an elite-managed distributive issue centering on specific interest-group demands, and later as a largely bureaucratic regulatory issue

51

involving negotiation between advocates and
administrators. The framework also draws out the
implications of comparable worth's potential as a
redistributive issue as critical events affect political
relationships and make elite management and
negotiation--whether interest group or
bureaucratic--difficult and costly. Theodore Lowi's
arenas of power and Richard Elmore's bargaining model of
implementation contribute to the framework.[1] The
theoretical dimensions will be outlined briefly, followed
by their application.

THEORETICAL DIMENSIONS OF
THE ANALYTIC FRAMEWORK

Lowi posits that political relationships are
determined by the kind of policy at stake. His three
major policy types--distributive, regulatory, and
redistributive--are characterized by specific political
relationships, power structures, and political processes
that he calls "arenas of power."

The earliest stages of comparable worth's
development were characterized by the elite definition of
the issue that directed interest-group attention to, and
participation in, a number of agenda-setting activities.
The politics were pluralist but elite dominated.

Pluralism is generally defined within the context of
democratic theory. It is narrower than classical
democratic theory and concerns who actually participates
in decision making rather than who might or who should.[2]
Proponents of pluralism describe it as a process in which
democratic values are preserved by political elites who
are held accountable to citizens through public opinion
or elections, or to institutions, organized interest
groups, and political parties through bargaining and
mutual accommodation. Pluralism assumes the
fragmentation of power in society. Access for new elites
exists within a framework of transitory power that shifts
from "group to group issue by issue."[3] The institutional
response to pressure from elite actors results in
treating issues as distributive policies, with bargaining
among elites over small discrete claims and benefits.

Lowi's examples of distributive arenas of
policymaking are pork-barrel legislation, services for
constituents, and patronage matters. Such policies tend
to stabilize conflict among coalitions of institutional
actors, such as representatives, distributive agencies,
and clientele groups by disaggregating decisions and
doling out benefits piecemeal.

"The door to the benefits is open to all," but the key dimension is elite influence with certain primary decision makers.[4] Distributive policies are low key and privately negotiated, or advanced through legislative logrolling. Decisions are made by so few people that even bureaucrats may be unaware of what is involved in some issues.[5] Because there is general consensus among institutional actors on the social value of the benefits, and no linkage or interference with the plans of others, costs remain less obvious and immediate, and conflict low.

In the earlier cases of legislative enactment of comparable worth studies, swift movement of the policy through state legislatures may well have been a natural response of lawmakers to treat the issue with distributive mechanisms, to oblige women legislators or union lobbyists by giving them their "innocuous" job evaluation studies as a logrolling gesture. These same mechanisms may also have operated in some local jurisdictions as well. Assessing "gains" within a pluralist framework requires thinking in terms of process, that is, attention is paid to the procedures used to facilitate change rather than to the substantive outcomes.[6] Pluralist analysis involves how changes are sought, not what changes are made.

In contrast, Lowi's model for regulatory policymaking involves contests between interest groups or sets of claimants and regulatory agencies. Policies regarding labor relations or agency administrative rule making are typical examples. Here individual decisions aggregate into precedents. Affirmative action and equal employment opportunity (EEO) policies fall into this category on the state and local levels. In many instances the interest-group liberalism of lawmakers gave a prominent place in implementation and oversight of comparable worth program execution to comparable worth advocates.[7] Once into implementation, the emphasis is not on logrolling or solely political incentives but on regulatory policies and bureaucratic incentives.

Historically, regulatory politics predominantly concerned economic issues, with close relationships between the regulated and regulator. Many political scientists tell us that regulatory issues have moved on to broader concerns, adopting procedures that insure more open political processes. Craig finds that "policymaking for governmental regulatory /functions now must operate/ in a more open and competitive pluralistic arena." Does this lead to more intergroup coalition building, bargaining, and compromise for legislators? No, says Craig, "on the contrary, either because /they are/ unable

to deal with the complex and highly technological issues
involved or because of the urgent need to develop a
consensus . . . /legislators have/ increasingly
transferred regulatory decisionmaking to the
administrative agencies."[8] This is certainly true for
labor relations and affirmative action-EEO, where all
authority for accommodation is delegated in most states
and large cities save for the final appropriation
decision.

The arena of power shifts in regulatory politics to
the agencies and bureaucratic politics.

As government became involved in new and
different aspects of economic and social life during
the twentieth century, the locus and character of
constituency representation changed. While
legislative constituencies remained significant, a
new kind of relationship began to evolve at the
administrative level. Indeed, the continued
well-being and growth of some...agencies became
linked more to servicing their constituents than to
anything else.[9]

The impact of regulatory policies is specific to a
designated industry, sector, or group, and conflict can
be intense. This is particularly true where there is a
low level of societal consensus on an issue or where
those being regulated have the will and the resources to
fight back. For instance, where state governments
receive regulatory edicts from the federal government,
they engage in calculative behavior, assessing the risks
of noncompliance.[10] The agency that has to administer
regulatory policies survives through its ability to
"technicize and bureaucratize decisions."[11] If those
regulated cannot bring about the agency's acquiescence to
their desire, they will try repeatedly to "capture" an
agency or kill it.[12]

In state after state, comparable worth advocates
became involved with the ongoing work of personnel
departments, developing guidelines and overseeing
execution of job evaluation studies. The power
structures they dealt with were not legislative bodies
but administrators; the emphasis was no longer on
logrolling or solely political incentives but regulatory
policies and bureaucratic incentives.

Although the number of groups coming to understand
comparable worth or to define it grew throughout the late
1970s, its politics remained elite dominated,
bureaucratic, and technical, contained within
administrative boundaries. As Elmore might have

predicted, in arenas of conflict, where bargaining
becomes the model of implementation, no stable or
permanent results are ever reached, except for strong
pressure by both sides to maintain the bargaining arena
to gain things of value to each.[13]

Because of its technical nature, comparable worth
could have remained fairly exclusively defined or
contained by either political elites desiring it or
administrators charged with executing legislative
studies. However, litigation produced a shock effect.

The ruling in _American Federation of State, County
and Municipal Employees_ v. _The State of
Washington_--almost $1 billion due in back wages and
benefits--moved comparable worth from an elite-dominated,
pluralist, or bureaucratic phenomenon to an issue that
has received broad media dramatization and enhancement
for community consumption. The media treatment may have
changed how the issue is defined and by whom. If
comparable worth is perceived as no longer a distributive
or regulatory issue but one involving mass mobilization
and redistribution, then power relationships and arenas
of conflict will similarly shift.

Redistributive policy issues invoke new conditions
and processes for relations among interests, and between
interests and government. Lowi finds redistributive
policies affect broad categories of citizens. The
associated, often intense conflict is generally fought
out on ideological grounds, reaching formal agenda status
easily because the potential impact more closely follows
class lines and interests.[14] In redistributive policies
there are generally two sides who have clear, stable, and
consistent interaction, with peak associations arising to
fulfill this role. Peak associations are generally more
effective when the issues are generalizable and
ideological demands are made.[15]

Other Elements. In addition to the three policy
types accommodating comparable worth's ascent on the
political agenda, three other components had to be in
place. First, the resources of the actors--the groups
desiring change in the economic status of
women--initially had to conform to the requirements of a
pluralist, incremental decision setting. The actors had
to socialize the conflict within manageable bounds by
gathering allies and redefining the issues. Second, the
environment to be changed, i.e., the public personnel
system, had to be susceptible to the displacement of
conflict because of organizational weakness. Third, the
interest-group liberalism of lawmakers and administrators
had to give a prominent place in implementation and

oversight of program execution to advocates.

Agenda setting used in its broadest sense includes analysis of emergent policy systems designed to act on problems on a continuing basis.[16] A major question of who is advantaged by which strategies under which conditions must be considered. The examples offered in this chapter complement both the pluralist and regulatory policy types. The questions raised by the examples are whether legislation that reduces conflict in the policymaking stages increases biases during implementation toward groups with well-defined interests and access or bargaining advantages,[17] or empowers other entities such as administrators,[18] or the courts.

Resources. Gelb and Palley's study of the role of women in American politics provides a set of rules to which emergent groups must conform to achieve even limited social change. The groups must be perceived as legitimate, and, to appear so, must focus on incremental, narrowly defined issues that do not portend sweeping societal changes (especially role changes, in the case of women). They must provide information, avoid confrontation, and mobilize allies. Finally, they must expand or contract their definition of an issue, and manipulate symbols favorable to it to contain it within manageable bounds. Generally, the broader the goals sought and the more visible the issue, the more that prevailing values seem threatened and countermovements arise to contest change. Gelb and Palley adjudge the most successful examples of issue attainment in the policymaking setting to have been when feminists conformed to the scope and bias of the system, and participated in coalition building around single issues organized by reformist leaders who generated an image of competence and broad-based support. A significant factor in the organizational life of national feminist groups, according to Gelb and Palley, is the increasing staff dominance of most boards in "selecting of issues and employing tactics and strategies for political influence."[19]

Gelb and Palley offer an excellent description of the intersection of feminism as a social movement and the organizational behavior of private interest groups supporting women's issues that lobby for social change. Their profiles of behavioral patterns, however, must be adapted to organizational settings in which the legitimacy of the participation of women's advocacy groups is altered by institutionalization through government action. On the state level, the incorporation of women's advocacy groups within agencies, such as commissions on the status of women, has transformed the

behavioral pattern; it has moved from the solely
legislative focus of nongovernmental groups that
concentrate on mobilizing political resources to the more
sophisticated administrative agency "inside-access" model
of policy development that has been described as the
"easiest and /most successful way for/ achieving both
formal agenda status and implementation of...policy."[20]

It is the elevation to agency status, and the
increasing dominance of the boards of state commissions
on the status of women by professional staff that has
altered the traditional policy framework and
interest-group strategies. The staffs of the commissions
are assuming leadership roles in selecting issues,
forming administrative constituencies,[21] and employing
tactics and strategies.

The institutionalization of women's advocacy groups
within state agencies has also facilitated the purposive
interaction of women legislator caucuses with many of
the groups, including public-sector unions. Unions have
sought liaisons with professional staffs of state
commissions and have become participants in feminist
policy planning networks. While friendships and shared
ideological concerns strengthen the linkages among these
groups,[22] the dominant factor in orchestrating
legislative action and planning implementation strategies
has been the availability of slack resources of the
professional staffs of the state commissions.[23] The staff
assumes the role of political entrepreneur, noted by
Walker, in formulating problems and mobilizing attention
to ideas whose "time has come."[24] Further, the staff
provides the legal and technical information to feminist
lawmakers who seek women legislator caucus support to
influence fellow lawmakers.[25] One additional resource of
the actors in bringing about adoption of new public
personnel policies is the defusing of a potentially
divisive issue such as comparable worth through labeling
to stress its technical nature[26] and the rallying of
influential allies who can stress its pragmatic nature.[27]

Characteristics of the Environment. Public
personnel administration has problems of image and
control. Even friendly critics call its operations
"impersonal, slow, unresponsive, rigid and expensive,"
and say it "scarcely accomplishes public employment
objectives."[28] Traditionally, personnel managers have
not been public advocates of equity issues; their
behavior is set by allegiance to the customary principles
of neutrality and objectivity in administration.
Legislative belief systems further reinforce the notion
that the work of public personnel administration is
apolitical and procedural rather than conflict ridden and

valuative.

But just as "organizational arrangements are not neutral" in the public sector,[29] neither are procedures and the rigor with which they are enforced. Insufficient guidelines exist in public personnel administration to assist managers in responsibly administering highly politicized systems. Indeed, managers who strive for organizational effectiveness by studying their own operations may find themselves selectively punished by adversaries who use the improved information generated as political currency in a contest for control.

Environmental factors are of paramount importance for public personnel. Three subgroups identified by Klinger--managers, employees, and outside groups--hold conflicting values and objectives relative to the operation of the system, and affect its survival in crucial ways. Legislators, courts, and regulatory agencies all influence the system in its labor relations functions. Most controversies involving conflicting objectives of competing subgroups have discredited the traditional assumptions "that personnel activities are routine and noncontroversial."[30]

Personnel theorists considering structural and behavioral impediments to civil service reforms relative to women see many environmental dilemmas to be addressed. Friss identifies four: (1) The need for management flexibility, balanced against the competing need for "adequate guidelines to safeguard and prevent abuse of the merit system." (2) The need to safeguard objectivity, or, where subjective factors play a major role in processes, to scrutinize them for conformity to larger equity principles. Few argue for greater politicization of the system, but "some activists fear increased rationalization would be manipulated by those now in control and would cement existing distortions" to the disadvantage of women. (3) The growing role of unions in determining pay policies is particularly pertinent to feminist concerns that male-dominated unions may block changes in job evaluation practices and criteria to safeguard their advantaged position. (4) The dominance of market factors plays unevenly on female-dominated occupations. Exceptions exist: public employers usually pay more than private to blue-collar workers, less to management and professional workers, and the same low wages to those in nursing, according to Friss; so, by itself, the market rationale seems ambiguous when applied.[31]

APPLICATION OF THE FRAMEWORK:
THE CONNECTICUT CASE

Policy analysis is used to probe the degree of fit of the theoretical framework to the development of comparable worth, assessing the impact of multiple strategies of agenda setting and implementation by advocacy coalitions. Policy analysis is helpful in offering benchmarks by which to judge the importance of social change. Limited in that it centers on whether issues in immediate contexts are resolved,[32] it nevertheless can highlight the normative dimension of issues.[33]

The analysis to follow describes features of agenda-setting processes in one state: the symbolization employed, especially labeling, and the character of the resources available to agenda setters to follow through with organizational incentives to insure implementation. It conforms to both the pluralist and bureaucratic models offered in the analytic framework.

The Connecticut case conforms to what Cobb, Ross, and Ross call the "inside access model" of policy development.[34] By using the professional staff of the Permanent Commission on the Status of Women to develop legislative and interest group constituencies, and to confine expansion to particularly influential groups, proponents achieved both formal agenda status and enhanced possibilities of implementation. For sponsors of very controversial issues, any legislative enactment that grants program status offers a better middle-range strategy than mobilization of a mass constituency.

The politically relevant context of the decision setting is critical to applying the policy framework to the Connecticut case. Context is understood to be an entire situation or environment pertaining to a particular event. To trace the progression of comparable worth from doctrine to policy and from policy to administration, it is necessary first to describe and explain the context that informed the successive decisions and then to relate the events that flowed from the inside-access model of policy development and implementation.

Two organizational factors were part of the context of the decision setting and the development of strategies. The first factor was the noteworthy organizational change within the Permanent Commission on the Status of Women. The PCSW, created in 1972, was brought from leaderless disarray and contention over operating style and mission[35] to a cohesive, advocacy agency professionally directed toward political activism.[36] The second factor was a series of organizational constraints on the policy formation and operations of the Department of Personnel and Labor Relations (DPLR). One constraint was the institution of collective bargaining in 1975. The legislation (PA-75-566), which came as a surprise to many observers, was hastily passed and then implemented on very short notice.[37] Another constraint was a general reorganization of state government in 1977 that delivered administrative aftershocks. The confluence of the two events made the DPLR director prone to accommodate legislative requests, or at least prone to exercise extreme caution in regard to any personnel issue to which lawmakers were attentive. The context, then, was in part composed of the organizational renaissance of the PCSW, which adopted the inside-access model to structure events, and the organizational vulnerability of the DPLR, which reacted circumspectly to events.

The chronology of events begins in the mid-1970s with constituent complaints to State Senator Audrey Beck by women employed by the State of Connecticut. They were unhappy over low pay; absence of career mobility, counseling, or training opportunities; and threats to job security for protesting perceived inequities. Beck and another feminist senator, Betty Hudson, diligently pursued each complaint with the employing agencies to try to reach some agreement on the points at issue administratively. The situation ballooned, however, as conferences with discontented individuals turned into lunches for roomsful of people, then into large meetings, joined by the new public-sector unions that were seeking constituencies and issues.

In 1975 Susan Bucknell was appointed executive director of the Permanent Commission on the Status of Women, bringing to it an activist orientation. The PCSW embarked on a study of state clerical workers,[38] aided by the Connecticut State Employees Association (CSEA), which had achieved union status with PA 75-566. After a number of public meetings and many conferences with personnel in state agencies and the DPLR, Beck found she could not untangle where responsibility for the women's complaints rested--with the agencies or with DPLR rule making; all disclaimed responsibility. She then concluded that legislative action was needed to address the problems of dead-end jobs and lack of career incentives, and drafted the "Upward Mobility Program" bill (PA 77-250) to initiate "creative administrative remedies" for bureaucratic intransigence.[39] The bill contained no appropriation provision nor any tangible incentives or guidelines for implementation but soon incurred union hostility, and was abandoned by Beck and other sponsors after two years.

Bucknell served on the multi-agency Upward Mobility Program study committee and wrote its report,[40] two activities that established her visibility and pattern of interaction with various successive study and advisory committees and evaluation task forces. Slack resources in the Connecticut case were Bucknell's time, opportunity, and desire to serve. They allowed her to operate the PCSW like a single-issue constituency, selecting legislative issues to research and lobby for, and mobilizing allies to achieve policy objectives. Bucknell had secured a position of independence relative to the appointed PCSW board of commissioners, and was free of its direction. Not encumbered with administering programs, as were other agency directors, she assumed leadership roles and gained considerable expertise on selected issues. She was particularly adept in the area of employment issues, and became a close working partner of women union lobbyists. What is compelling about the relationship--each acting for her group in an agency-clientele relationship--is its resemblance to an administrative constituency.[41]

As Gelb and Palley note, incentives for feminist leaders in political settings are as Robert Salisbury described them, both ideological and social. "Individuals are drawn into the movement's network by ideology and often personal relationships, and they remain part of the complex organizational structure through extensive contacts, networks, and social ties."[42] When the Upward Mobility Program failed to achieve its sponsors' purposes after two years of administrative study, it was natural that Beck looked to Bucknell and union activists for a new direction. One union leader, Betty Tianti, had been a close friend, early supporter, and one-time campaign manager of Beck's, and as primary lobbyist for the AFL-CIO had considerable contact with Bucknell. Incentives beyond social considerations, for Beck, were straightforward. She believed in pay equity for women, had been thwarted in trying to produce administrative remedies, and needed continuing union financial and lobbying support for a number of other legislative issues.

No one now can recall who initiated comparable worth as a logical next step; it seems simply to have arisen in a discussion among Beck, Hudson, Bucknell, and Tianti and other union activists who were contemplating the imminent demise of the Upward Mobility Program. How to construct a bill with safeguards such as to make implementation actually possible? Someone brought up the State of

Washington's experience with comparable worth, and the
concept caught on with the group. Bucknell believes Beck
then asked her to get a copy of the Washington
legislation regarding the objective job evaluation study.
The bill Bucknell later wrote and had introduced called
for the direct implementation of changes in the
classification system, which Beck subsequently changed in
committee testimony to a study of the classification
system. After this false start, the legislation and
strategies appear to have reached maturity through a
number of planning meetings that involved two more union
lobbyists (Sylvia Terrill, CSEA; and Debby King, Local
1199, a hospital and health care workers union). Out of
the meetings, which began before and continued through
the 1979 legislative session, came a coalition that could
lobby and marshal support for the bill. Bargaining and
litigation--to raise the stakes for governmental
inaction-- were later assumed by the unions.

The issue moved directly to the policy arena, where
labeling and intense lobbying made objective job
evaluation "a mainstream political issue." As Bucknell
was to tell the national Women's Conference on Pay Equity
five months later, "1298 /Senate bill number for PA
79-72/ never had a vote against it."⁴³ The coalition
worked. Bucknell's account of the strategy and outcome
is instructive:

> The administration was not
> enthusiastic about the bill. The major
> unions and the AFL-CIO were in support of
> the bill. The CSEA supported SB 1298 as
> part of their agreeing not to oppose a
> management bill that the Personnel
> Director wanted. This deal was the key to
> getting and maintaining administration
> support. The clericals lobbied in such a
> way that legislators recognized this as a
> constituent issue. We could not have
> gotten the bill out of the labor committee
> without the chair's support /also an
> AFL-CIO person/. It could not have been
> lobbied through without strong labor
> support, not only CSEA,...but also the
> state AFL-CIO, whose chief lobbyist was a
> woman (Tianti), and the campaign manager
> for the woman legislator (Beck) who had
> been the original supporter. . . .

> The PCSW's role was also important.
> We were in a position to constantly
> research and answer questions. What would
> it mean to have an objective basis for

evaluation or rating jobs? What was
comparable worth? How much would it cost?
We were also able to bring together the
various parties and mediate and
communicate between the parties. . . .

Her prognosis of outcome was equally precise:

Our route to monitoring the study and
the implementation is an advisory
committee. The membership includes the
major unions and advocates for the bill
and others recommended by the Director of
Personnel. We see the continued coalition
of the various forces as crucial in
addressing real conflicts that the study
and implementation could raise. . . .

Her conclusions:

The work is only just begun.
Legislation is only one strategy to
achieve objective job evaluation. It does
have an advantage as an organizing tool.
People can focus on a bill. It may well
be...that the most satisfactory result of
objective job evaluation is the stronger
organization of clericals themselves. It
also depends on the existence of other
strategies such as court cases. I think
the ultimate success in Connecticut...will
depend on the extent to which we mesh
these various strategies.[44]

Introducing comparable worth under the label of
objective job evaluation, its methodological rather than
doctrinal "face,"[45] effectively converted a potentially
controversial issue into a "motherhood" issue.
Employment, equity, parity, and women's rights are
explicitly controversial, but affixing a technical label
to the issue directed attention to its potential for
personnel reform through scientific management
mechanisms. Scientific or technical issues are less
likely than social issues to be hotly debated because
they seem amenable to mechanistic solutions.[46]

The outcomes included three studies that passed the
Connecticut legislature: the 1979 Pilot Objective Job
Evaluation Study, PA 79-72 referenced above; the 1980
Classification Study; and the 1981 Objective Job
Evaluation, which called for a large survey and
subsequent analysis of 2,500 job classes. An advisory
committee structure was implanted to guide the studies,

and its membership included several advocates (Bucknell, PCSW; Tianti, AFL-CIO; and King, Local 1199) as well as eleven union representatives, four public and two private personnel managers, and two legislators representing the Labor Committee. The same consultant was hired for all three studies: Norman D. Willis and Associates, who had conducted the State of Washington studies, and who was the choice of the advocates on the committee.

The first study's findings indicated there might be some faulty aspects to the classification system, that in some classes pay and skill levels were not commensurate with responsibility, and jobs staffed predominately by women paid 8 to 18 percent less than those staffed by men. Willis recommended further study, as well as the implementation of the concept of comparable worth to achieve greater equity.[47] The second study concluded that the classification system was not operating as poorly as had been suggested in the pilot study. The third study, authorized in June 1981, was to have completed gathering data by 1984 but was extended two years. A full-time DPLR staff person, Barbara Waters, was named director of a new Objective Job Evaluation Unit. She had experience in DPLR and good working relations with the PCSW and union representatives.

A month after the passage of the bill instituting the third objective job evaluation study, the U.S. Supreme Court opened the way for sex-based wage discrimination claims, such as those using comparable worth factors as standards of proof under Title VII. In County of Washington v. Gunther (1981) it ruled that appeals under Title VII's broad prohibitions against discrimination no longer had to meet the narrow tests of equal pay for equal work of the EPA. Although the court explicitly did not base its opinion on comparable worth, it nonetheless did rule that women who hold different jobs than do men can file discrimination charges.[48]

In July 1981, the American Federation of State, County and Municipal Employees (AFSCME), which would be contending with CSEA to represent state clerical employees, joined an existing CSEA suit filed in federal court in 1979. The remedy asked for was $300 million. AFSCME, using data from the objective job evaluation studies, charged inequality of "rates of pay which defendants /the State of Connecticut/ have determined to be of comparable or equal value to work performed by male employees at higher rates of pay."[49]

Elsewhere, AFSCME engaged in strike action in the City of San Jose, California, again citing objective job evaluation study findings, and also filed suit against

the State of Washington. In San Jose, the political
environment was conducive to immediate remedy, and the
feminist-dominated city council provided a settlement
that included $1.45 million in pay adjustments for women
found to be in undervalued positions. The suit in
Connecticut is still pending.   Its one immediate effect
has been to curtail administrative comment on the
progress of the current study while the earlier findings
are under litigation. The Advisory Committee is
routinely briefed on the progress of the study, and
retains its character as a resource for the
implementation goals of the advocates. Resources to
complete the study in Connecticut have become more
abundant, and the study was extended to 1986.
Male-dominated electrical and maintenance unions,
however, have refused to complete job surveys. And
negotiation continues.

COMPARABLE WORTH'S PROBABLE EFFECTS
ON PERSONNEL ADMINISTRATION

Outcomes of the policy process have to be analyzed
along two dimensions: by the events immediately apparent
in the instant case, and by the probable long-term
effects of the framework applied elsewhere.

The skillful displacement of the conflict originally
concerned with pay equity for women onto public
personnel's classification practices and systems is
difficult to analyze systematically and to draw
generalizations from for prediction.   It is correct that
not everyone is equally implicated or influential in the
policy implementation process.   It is also correct that
analysts should study the resources and leverage
potential of a small group of policymaking actors whose
roles are central to agenda setting.[50] But, the
assumption that an individual or group has leverage
throughout the life of an issue--initiation to
implementation--fails to take into account the strategies
and constraints that administrative organizations
themselves employ as they define and pursue political
objectives and cope with the environment.[51] As Bardach
suggests, at the level of description the "political
dynamics of the implementation process resemble the
dynamics of the policy adoption process."[52] But
similarity of process does not mean that the symbolic and
practical institutional, social, or personal resources of
political actors in policy initiation translate into
organizational incentives in program delivery, or
implementation.

Personnel systems, as organizations, have varying
incentive systems, and act individualistically to meet

their maintenance and enhancement needs.[53] Differences
in historical origin, and in the social and political
structures in which personnel systems are embedded, as
well as their perceptions of their organizational
autonomy or vulnerability, facilitate or retard
implementation. Political actors influential in agenda
setting may well affect the incentive structure of an
implementing organization and subsequently intervene in
its technological processes. Such intervention, though,
depends directly upon having two sets of resources:
political, meaning those relevant to policy settings; and
organizational, meaning those relevant to implementation.

On the theoretical level there is wide disagreement
over the efficacy and desirability of continuous
intervention in all stages of the policy process from
initiation to implementation. Bardach sees a more
interactive role for those who set the agenda. He wants
them to become involved, as participants, in the
continuous, successive modifications of program and
policy that he believes implementation requires.[54]
Bardach foresees a continuous intervention by the
original sponsors of legislation. Vagueness of statutory
authority for instance, is not necessarily an
insurmountable problem. Lowi, contrariwise, insists that
vague legislation increases biases during implementation
toward groups with well-defined interests and access.
According to Lowi, few standards of implementation
accompany delegation of power to administrators, and he
hypothesizes that a public philosophy of interest-group
liberalism has arisen to justify participation of groups
in governance, and delegation of authority from lawmaking
bodies to administrators.[55] The effect is rationalization
of access for privileged groups, and the undermining of
accountability.

Pressman and Wildavsky suggest that the failure of
policies to achieve anything close to the goals of
original sponsors is attributable to the "divorce of
implementation from policy."[56] Where Lowi calls for more
specificity in legislation and withdrawal of
interest-group participation in implementation, Bardach
envisions laws that purposively facilitate intervention
by sponsors to adjust the idealized goals of the
initiation stage to the practical realities of the
implementation process. Lowi's concern is that democratic
principles will be violated by the privileged access of
nonrepresentative groups. Bardach's concern is more
process oriented: patterns of underperformance, delay,
and escalating costs occur unless sponsors "set policy
back on course" during implementation.[57]

Stakes of the Actors. Several practical matters certainly affect whether original sponsors of objective job evaluation studies can successfully intervene and direct, or bargain for advantages, during implementation in Connecticut and other jurisdictions. Three potential constraints involve nongovernmental actors: organized ad hoc groups of antifeminists, the business community, and public-sector unions that represent male constituencies. The antifeminists represent a threat to further diffusion of comparable worth on the state and local levels. If they escalate the conflict by successfully labeling it a redistributive issue,[58] it would no longer be able to be handled routinely. Timing here is critical,[59] for if enough states are willing to carry out implementation, opposition will be undermined.

The business community and male-dominated unions both have a material interest in the wage structure and classification systems in the public sector. Although the national AFL-CIO is on record as supporting comparable worth, its stand bespeaks the 1979 lobbying of the Coalition of Labor Union Women at a national convention more than the operational acceptance by the male public-sector rank and file, who must base future wage demands on what is likely to be a diminishing resource base. More women members is a rational objective for national and local unions, and feminist authors increasingly depict unions as vehicles for accelerating social change in the workplace.[60] But public employers will be hard pressed either to continue funding blue-collar, male-dominated union demands at current levels or to increase compensation for predominately sex-segregated female occupations. It is likely that public and private management will find greater merit in a heavier machine-person mix for activities that women traditionally handle than in financially committing themselves to a potentially restive work force.

The next two chapters survey what has happened in other states. Many states resemble the Connecticut model, that is, incremental policies proposing objective job evaluation studies were suggested to streamline personnel operations, as well as to review factor weights in classifications schemes for relevance to organizational purposes and for possible bias. Proponents stress the technical nature of the issue, and that conflict is over management practices.

Although it is difficult to predict how comparable worth has developed in all settings because of the lack of case studies like the Connecticut case, two things are clear: economic issues are the new agenda in politics for women; and, with unionization, public personnel administration has no readily apparent constituencies to bolster its claims to legitimacy as apolitical representatives of neutral employment policies. One conclusion seems clear from even a cursory study of environmental factors: Public personnel systems, as organizations, should pay close attention to survival concerns and environmental factors as they try to reach consensus on goals, objectives, and practices. Through the growth of incompatible goals, incremental policies, subgroup politics, and archaic practices, the systems have become the likeliest target for issue displacement and further politicization.

NOTES

1. T. Lowi, "American Business, Public Policy Case Studies and Political Theory," World Politics 16 (1963), pp. 677-715; R. Elmore, "Organizational Models of Social Program Implementation," Public Policy 26 (Spring 1978), pp. 185-228; and T. Lowi, "Four Systems of Policy, Politics, and Choice," Public Administration Review 32 (1972), pp. 298-310.
2. T.R. Dye and L.H. Zeigler, The Irony of Democracy (Belmont, CA, 1971), pp. 8-19.
3. D. Stewart, The Women's Movement: Community Politics in the United States (New York, 1980), p. 101.
4. G.L. Wamsley and M.N. Zald, The Political Economy of Public Organizations (Bloomington, IN, 1973), pp. 36-37.
5. R.W. Cobb and C.D. Elder, Participation in American Politics (Boston, 1972), p. 95. Elsewhere "logrolling" is defined by S.M. Morehouse as involving "a group giving support to a proposal that may bear no relation or only the remotest relation to its own objectives in return for similar support from the group it has assisted." State Politics, Parties, and Policy (New York, 1980), p. 141.
6. Stewart, Women's Movement, p. 103.
7. Interest-group liberalism is defined in the Introduction, footnote 12.
8. B. Craig, "The Legislative Veto: Its Implications for Administration and the Democratic Process" (Ph.D. diss., University of Connecticut, 1982). See also M. Lepper, "Affirmative Action: A Tool for Effective Personnel Management," in Public Personnel Administration, ed. S. Hays and R. Kearney (Englewood Cliffs, NJ, 1983), p. 220. Lepper believes afirmative action is a redistributive policy that has lacked

application but offers no evidence to support her judgment.

9. E. Lewis, American Politics in a Bureaucratic Age (Cambridge, MA, 1977), p. 12.

10. Wamsley and Zald, Political Economy of Public Organizations, pp. 36-37.

11. D.S. Wright, Understanding Intergovernmental Relations, 2d ed. (Monterey, CA, 1982), p. 72.

12. M. Edelman, The Symbolic Uses of Politics (Urbana, 1967), pp. 5,56,74; R.G.Noll, "The Behavior of Regulatory Agencies," Review of Social Economy 29 (March 1981), pp. 18-19.

13. Elmore, "Organizational Models of Social Program Implementation," p. 219.

14. Wamsley and Zald, Political Economy of Public Organizations, pp. 36-37.

15. Lowi, "American Business, Public Policy Case Studies and Political Theory," p. 709.

16. L.D. Hoppe, "Agenda Setting Strategies: Pollution Policy," cited in C.S. Jones, An Introduction to the Study of Public Policy (North Scituate, MA, 1977).

17. M. Derthick, New Towns in Town (Washington, DC, 1970).

18. H. Kaufman, Red Tape: Its Origin, Uses, and Abuses (Washington, DC, 1977); H. Seidman, Politics, Position, and Power, 2d ed. (New York, 1980); L.L. Jaffe, Judicial Control of Administrative Action (Boston, 1965); K.C. Davis, Administrative Law Treatise (St. Paul, 1970).

19. J. Gelb and M.L. Palley, Women and Public Policies (Princeton, 1982), pp. 5, 11, 38, 42, 170.

20. R. Cobb, J.-K. Ross, and M.H. Ross, "Agenda Building as a Comparative Political Process," American Political Science Review 70 (March 1976), pp. 126-38.

21. P. Selznick, TVA and the Grass Roots (Berkeley, 1949).

22. Gelb and Palley, Women and Public Policies, p. 170.

23. "Slack resources" is used in B.Nelson, "Setting the Public Agenda: The Case of Child Abuse," in The Policy Cycle, ed. J. May and A.B. Wildavsky (Beverly Hills, 1978), to refer to organizational resources available to political actors by virtue of position. Such resources also include time, opportunity, and ambition.

24. J.L. Walker, "Setting the Agenda in the U.S. Senate: A Theory of Problem Selection," British Journal of Political Science 7 (October 1977), pp. 423-45.

25. Gelb and Palley, Women and Public Policies, p. 170. top 26. Nelson, "Setting the Public Agenda," p.35.

27. Gelb and Palley, Women and Public Policies, p. 170.

28. C.A. Newland, "Public Personnel Administration: Legalistic Reforms v. Effectiveness, Efficiency and

Economy," _Public Administration Review_ 36 (September/October 1976), pp. 529-537.

29. Seidman, _Politics, Position, and Power_.

30. D.E. Klinger, "Political Influences on the Design of State and Local Personnel Systems," _Review of Public Personnel Administration_ 1 (Summer 1981), p. 2.

31. L. Friss, "Equal Pay for Comparable Worth: Stimulus for Future Civil Service Reform," _Review of Public Personnel Administration_ 2 (Summer 1982), pp. 44-45.

32. K.W. Kramer, "Seeds of Success and Failure: Policy Development and Implementation of the 1978 Civil Service Reform Act," _Review of Public Personnel Administration_ 2 (Spring 1982), pp. 5-20.

33. E. Johansen, "Managing the Revolution: The Case of Comparable Worth," _Review of Public Personnel Administration_, 4 (Spring 1984), p. 17.

34. Cobb, Ross, and Ross, "Agenda Building as a Comparative Political Process."

35. J.D. Oldfield, "A Case Study on the Impact of Public Policy Affecting Women," _Public Administration Review_ 36 (July-August 1976), pp. 385-89.

36. Interview with Susan Bucknell, executive director, Permanent Commission on the Status of Women, State of Connecticut, 27 January 1982.

37. S. Biloon, "Collective Bargaining in Connecticut: Some Good News and Some Bad News," _Intergovernmental Personnel Notes_ (Office of Personnel Management), July-August 1979, pp. 17-20.

38. Connecticut Permanent Commission on the Status of Women, "Clerical Work: A Manual for Change." (Hartford, 1977).

39. Interview with State Senator Audrey Beck, January 26, 1982.

40. "Report of the Upward Mobility Committee to the Legislature," Hartford, 1979.

41. P. Selznick, _TVA and the Grass Roots_ (Berkeley, 1949). The chair of the PCSC in Connecticut is the political action director for the New England Health Care Employees Union, District 1199. For an interview summarizing her view of no conflict between the roles, see L. Bernstein, "Labor Leader Comfortable with Women's Commission Issues, " _Hartford Courant_, 29 November 1982, pp. B1-2.

42. Gelb and Palley, _Women and Public Policies_, p. 40.

43. S. Bucknell, "The Connecticut Story on Objective Job Evaluation," in _Manual on Pay Equity_, ed. J. A. Grune. (Washington, DC, 1980), pp. 125-28.

44. Ibid.

45. Helen Remick's analysis in 1980 of why the state of Washington's comparable worth activities had failed offers a prescription to other states: "If the

Washington experience is generalizable, it appears that once an evaluation system is touted as eliminating sex bias. . . it may be impossible to implement it." "Beyond Equal Pay for Equal Work: Comparable Worth in the State of Washington," in Equal Employment Policy for Women, ed. R. Ratner (Philadelphia, 1980), p. 418.

46. Nelson, "Setting the Public Agenda."

47. N.D. Willis and Associates, "Objective Job Evaluation Pilot Study" (Hartford, 1980).

48. S.M. Neuse, "A Critical Perspective on the Comparable Worth Debate," Review of Public Personnel Administration 3 (Fall 1982), pp. 1-20.

49. Connecticut State Employees Association (CSEA) v. State of Connecticut H-79-197 (D.Conn) Intervention petition filed by American Federation of State, County and Municipal Workers, p. 5.

50. K.J. Gergen, "Assessing the Leverage Points in the Process of Policy Formation," in The Study of Policy Formation, ed. R.A. Bauer and K.J. Gergen (New York, 1968), p. 181.

51. J.Q. Wilson, Political Organizations (Boston, 1973), p. 30.

52. E. Bardach, The Skill Factor in Politics: Repeal in the Mental Commitment Laws (Berkeley, 1972), pp. 241-61.

53. Wilson, Political Organizations, p. 30.

54. E. Bardach, "On Designing Implementable Programs," in Pitfalls of Analysis, ed. G. Majone and E.S. Quade (New York, 1980), pp. 138-58; E. Bardach, The Implementation Game: What Happens After a Bill Becomes a Law (Cambridge, 1977).

55. T. Lowi, The End of Liberalism (New York, 1969), p. 85.

56. J.L. Pressman and A.R. Wildavsky, Implementation: How Great Expectations in Washington Are Dashed in Oakland (Berkeley, 1983), p. 135.

57. Bardach, Implementation Game.

58. J.K. Boles, The Politics of the Equal Rights Amendment (New York, 1979), pp. 1-28, 61-93.

59. M.R. Daniels and R. Darcy, "As Time Goes By: The Arrested Diffusion of the Equal Rights Amendment," Publius (forthcoming, 1984), develop and test the hypothesis that the timing of a policy can largely determine its success or failure. The states that were slow in adopting the ERA became more vulnerable to the efforts of ad hoc groups who mastered the community conflict model to oppose ratification successfully. Daniels and Darcy note, "As the level of conflict increased some public officials backed off from active support and legislatures resorted to avoiding decisions" (p. 3).

60. A. Cook, "Collective Bargaining as a Strategy for Achieving Equal Opportunity and Equal Pay," in Equal

Employment Policy for Women, ed. R. Ratner (Philadelphia, 1980); J.W.Scott, "Mechanization of Women's Work," *Scientific American*, September 1982, pp. 166-87.

4
Where Changes Are Sought

INTRODUCTION

Generalizations are hard come by when dealing with where changes have been and are being sought. For instance, two women governors elected in their own right, Dixie Lee Ray of Washington and Ella Grasso of Connecticut, were in office when comparable worth initiatives were under way in their states.[1] Ray deleted a proposed $7 million inequity adjustment from her predecessor's budget, quipping that the consultant's methodology had compared "apples and pumpkins and cans of worms and they are not compatible." Grasso was uncustomarily silent and did not lend her considerable influence to the issue.[2]

Questions arise as to whether comparable worth has a nonrandom diffusion pattern, which might suggest innovativeness by states and localities or particular strengths of organized interest groups. Does the level of professionalism of state or local personnel operations, or the legislatures, facilitate or retard the appearance of comparable worth or its adoption and use? For instance, is a unionized work force a prerequisite? Or are policy adoptions random, unattributable to political culture or socioeconomic characteristics or regions?

One must ponder why women or those acting in women's behalf have increased their attention to state governments. Is this a spin-off of ratification activity in connection with the Equal Rights Amendment? Or is it due, perhaps, to the notion held by advocates that the states are more innovative or accessible?

Are the states more active than the federal government in experimenting with social legislation? Is that what is at issue here? Such was the case with civil

73

service reform, where the states outperformed the "feds."
Persuasive perhaps is that among those women who are
interested and active in government, the states are
generally perceived to be more accessible and innovative
than the federal government.[3] The rationale offered by
leaders in the pay equity movement follows this
perception. Carin Clause, Solicitor of the U.S.
Department of Labor, expressed it best at the Conference
on Pay Equity in Washington: "I would not like at this
point in time to fight in the federal Congress. I think
state legislation will help us. The more state laws we
can get, the better predicate we have for a federal law.
Very rarely in this field has the federal government been
first. The Equal Pay Act was passed when we had
twenty-nine states with equal pay laws. The Age Act was
passed when we had twenty-six states. The same with
Title VII. The federal Congress is not usually the
leader here."[4]

This chapter takes a close look at these several
factors. Central to its arguments is that the general
circumstances of governance in the states themselves
strongly contributed to the introduction of comparable
worth. It was not merely a "women's issue" or a "labor
issue" or a "personnel issue." It spread from state to
state because it was all of those issues and, more
important perhaps, a "management issue" as well. It
exampled an idea of accountability whose performance
seemed methodologically "do-able" and whose time had
come. The next section reviews those general aspects of
the changing role of state government that became crucial
for the intersection of civil service reform and
comparable worth. There follows a record of where the
pay equity movement occurred, and then some possible
explanations are offered.

THE CHANGING ROLE OF THE STATES
IN THE FEDERAL SYSTEM

The part played by the states in enhancing the
quality of life of citizens has become more prominent.[5]
Many states have had unusual combinations of
gubernatorial and party leadership, fiscal stability, and
modernized legislative and executive branch organizations
to command leverage in the intergovernmental policy game.
Still the forgotten level of government in the public
consciousness, too big or remote for direct citizen
involvement and loyalty,[6] most state governments
nonetheless have shed the negative image of fraud, waste,
or abuse. While perceptions of relative strength and
effectiveness are slow to change and are tied to the
demands of time and place,[7] the reality of governance in
the states over the last decade increasingly is one of

dynamism, engagement in moral issues, and high political drama.

By the 1970s the states emerged as powerful decision-making entities, addressing social issues that Vietnam had diverted from the national policy agenda. This trend continues in the 1980s.[8] The majority of the states have taken steps to insure that they are more than conduits for federal aid to localities, that indeed they are partners in governance with federal and local governments.[9] Their aggressiveness in raising revenues over the past thirty years at not quite double the rate of increase of the federal government is noteworthy. "From 1950 to 1979 national revenues increased by a multiple of nine and local revenues by a multiple of 12. State revenues, however, rose by more than 17 times, from $8.8 billion in 1950 to $151.0 billion in 1979." The role of the states in a wide array of policy areas similarly expanded.[10]

The capacities of states to govern--their sufficiency of resources, their mechanisms for standardizing practices, and their ability for generating good-will in the public--vary widely from state to state. What has remained constant across states in the last twenty years is a trend toward greater modernization and full-time engagement in every aspect of civic life. Legislatures that were biennial in the 1960s are now in the minority. By 1978 forty-three legislatures had adopted annual sessions, and twenty-eight had the capacity to self-convene special sessions.[11] Staff support for legislatures has become professionalized and more ample. Policy analysts were found only in a meager dozen legislative research agencies in the early 1960s, but by 1979 there were over 187 such agencies.[12] Lawmakers' salaries went up, countering high turnover. All these factors bolstered the idea of permanence.[13] Lobbyists have found year-round encampment in state capitols to be good political strategy.

In the years immediately following World War II, the state legislatures had been primarily rural hegemonies. The "porkchoppers," as they were called in Florida, were the classic example.[14] Before 1961 it took only 12.3 percent of the state's voting population to elect a majority to the Florida Senate, and 17 percent to elect a majority to the House. Those elected represented the sparsely settled rural North Florida constituencies.[15]

State legislatures in the 1950s and 1960s were accurately depicted as archaic organizations suffering from "institutional lag."[16] Change began with reapportionment in the late 1960s, and the momentum has not stopped. When Chief Justice Earl Warren said for the majority in Reynolds v. Sims that the equal protection clause meant that both houses of legislatures were to be apportioned on the basis of population, he made it clear that legislatures represented people, "not trees or acres. Voters, not farms or cities or economic interests."[17]

By 1968 one man, one vote had become the rule in practice. The Citizens Conference on State Legislatures (CCSL), an organization created to improve communication among the states, in a 1971 study evaluating several legislatures, suggested ways to enhance legislative effectiveness.[18] The areas needing improvement were informational tools, structure, procedures, and services to legislators. Subsequently many legislatures did reorganize: some through constitutional revision, others through rule changes. Professional staffing in forty legislatures increased 130 percent from 1968 to 1974, from 745 to 1,715 persons.[19]

The legislatures were not alone in bringing themselves up to date. Constitutional revision and reorganization were also becoming commonplace accompaniments for the modern governor, as was a revitalized two-party system.[20] The development of the executive budget, the ability to veto legislation, planning, management, and public relations tools made the governor's power in many states preeminent.

A cycle of recessions in 1957-58, 1960, 1969-70, and 1973-75 jolted the economies of the states and exacerbated the institutional lag of legislatures and state bureaucracies. Management skills, reporting systems, a capacity for prompt and accurate decision making, knowledge of intergovernmental mechanisms to capture and use the stream of resources moving from the federal level, the ability to shape and institutionalize relationships, and to keep the public informed all became essential accoutrements of power in the states.

Timeliness was currency in the new state governments, and the office of the governor was the natural counter of the slower and diffuse plural decision making of the legislature. Legislators worked through committee structures, using time for maneuvering to build consensus. They habitually gathered a good portion of their information from lobbyists or in public forums in the early 1970s.[21] The governor, in contrast, was singular and moved to be the chief executive in fact--often the party leader as well--seizing policy initiatives and commanding media attention.[22]

Representation by population had a synergistic
effect on the development of administrative agencies in
state government, accelerating the number and raising the
qualifications of employees.[23] Women made only modest
gains in agency-head status between 1964 and 1978,[24] but
their numbers doubled in the legislatures.[25] The nature
of administrative service changed in these decades as
well. The drive for more specialization, knowledge
experts, and higher levels of education was widespread.
Statistics on the qualifications of agency heads in 1964
and 1978 show a shift toward formal training. In 1964,
34 percent of the administrators had no college degree;
in 1978, 58 percent had graduate degrees, and the number
with no college had decreased to 11 percent.[26] The
specialties of these predominately white-male agency
heads were accounting, business, law, management, and
public administration.[27]

Specialization appears in the culture of legislators
and legislative staff people as well. Huwa and
Rosenthal's study of the work habits of legislators and
staffs shows that each group exhibits distinct
differences in its focus of attention and desired
concentration of energies.[28] Legislators want
measurement of the political aspects of issues or of the
potential impact on constituents or their own careers;
staff members are concerned more with the technical sides
of the issues. Legislators are oriented toward service,
generalizing experience and events, and conceptualizing
issues in terms of political criteria; staff members
remain rooted in the informational aspects of work.

Although forty states have undergone structural
reorganizations of their administrative frameworks in the
past twenty years, empirical assessments of the effect of
reorganization on productivity, administrative responsiveness, accountability, or the political relationships
between branches of government and the public are
sparse.[29] The paucity of studies is caused in part by
the practical difficulties of comparative political
research.[30] The complexity and speed of change, and dif-
ficulty of access to multiple sets of actors responsible
for decision making in the fifty states is formidable.

Several events in the 1970s created a general
climate that made the experience of public officials in
the states quite similar--although their cultural milieus
and responses might differ. The first was a general wave
of citizen-inspired reform activity directed toward
creating accountability through legislation concerning
campaign financing, open meetings or open records, and
ethics. Alexander reports that in the early 1970s
forty-four states took action "to reduce the influence of

money and secrecy in their political processes."[31]

The second event was the June 1978 adoption by California voters of the Jarvis-Gann initiative. Proposition 13, an initiative petition, placed a limitation on state and local property tax revenues. Its cost in lost revenues to local jurisdictions was $6 billion. Proposition 13 was to become a model for other citizen initiatives in other states. It is estimated that the California proposition "induced an overall national decline in property taxes of about $1 billion."[32] Proposition 13 foreshadowed a turning point of national importance as property tax reductions were quickly joined by fiscal and administrative stringencies in the 1980s created by the Reagan administration's redesigning of federal aid to the states.[33]

Tax relief was not all that the public had in mind with initiative petitions. In spring 1984, 155 initiative petition measures--ranging from capital punishment to revamping legislative rules--were introduced in nineteen states and the District of Columbia,[34] signaling once again the restiveness of the public with the politics, costs, and administration of the states.[35]

Most states came of age as political institutions in the 1970s. They had fought against, then acquiesced in representation on the basis of population. Modernity escalated organizational gamesmanship to a high art form among the major institutional participants in state politics: legislatures, governors, state agencies, and the political parties. Some states experienced real organizational change that generated new decision premises. Some attempts at change only dramatized power relationships that were unyielding, irrespective of pressure or need.

Comparable worth appeared in different forms and at different times in the several states. The growing representation of women in state legislatures, the institutionalization of women's interests within commissions on women, and the emergent unionization of the public sector all contributed to change.

DIFFUSION OF COMPARABLE WORTH AMONG THE STATES

There are logical and empirical pitfalls in developing a diffusion model for comparable worth. The assessment of the effect of economic, political, and social characteristics on the states' receptivity to new policies is widely researched and debated in political

science. There are several research traditions to choose
from. Diffusion theory and studies of innovativeness in
the states represent a major area. Subsets of this
tradition are studies focusing on political factors (such
as reapportionment, governor's power, legislative
professionalism, party competitiveness), on economic
factors (such as research on socioeconomic predictors of
legislative expenditures), and on social and cultural
factors (such as D. Elazar's impressionistic concept,
political culture, later quantified by I. Sharkansky).

Several of these were helpful in considering the
theoretical possibilities inherent in the diffusion of
comparable worth, especially the findings concerning the
incidence and diffusion of innovativeness of the states
by Walker, Gray, Welch, Daniels, Eyestone, and Savage.[36]
Most persuasive are the works of Gray and Daniels, each
of whom concludes that the process by which a new policy
moves or is "diffused" from state to state depends on at
least two things: the general tendency of a state to be
receptive to innovations, and the nature of the issue and
the time period in which it arises. Gray's findings
corroborate the earlier conclusions of Walker that
innovative states, at the time of policy adoption, tend
to be those that are wealthier and have higher levels of
party competition for the governorship.[37] However, Gray
rejects innovativeness as a pervasive characteristic of a
state, drawing the inference that "innovativeness is
issue and time specific, and should not be aggregated
over long time periods."[38]

Gray explores a possible "interaction effect"
whereby adopter states infuence those that have not yet
adopted a policy. The gain of adoptions, she finds, is
attributable in part to nonadopters' emulation of
adopters.[39] Walker finds merit in Gray's point, and
expands the interaction effect into two spheres: those
states that attune themselves to national trends (the
national leaguers), and those that take their cues and
exchange information in more regionalized arenas.[40]
Eyestone's findings complement these conclusions by
taking into account the particular politics of a state at
the time it considers the innovation. Three elements
emerge, then, to temper arguments of a pervasive
characteristic of innovativeness. These are that there
is assuredly a tendency toward innovativeness for some
states but that particular features of a policy, and the
timing and politics operating in a given state when it is
considered all mediate such a tendency and make it less
than absolute.

Gray's findings on the diffusion of civil rights
laws are most instructive for analysis of comparable

worth's diffusion: civil rights corroborated the phenomenon of innovativeness of states in her longitudinal study of three issues. The average of her states' rank intercorrelation with civil rights laws was .67. This was in keeping with her earlier findings of strong associations between the distribution of civil rights laws, and wealth and party competition of states. Her model additionally showed that "diffusion patterns do differ by issue area, and by degree of federal involvement."[41] Civil rights laws were the most politicized of the issues she considered. This has not been characteristic of comparable worth thus far, but may become so.

The next section covers the research of the author on where comparable worth has been diffused. Innovation theory will then be discussed again, in the context of the findings and in view of alternative theories.

INCIDENCE OF COMPARABLE WORTH:
A RESEARCH MODEL

The first task is to describe what is, and then speculate as to why comparable worth appeared as an issue where it did and subsequently developed or languished. Several general hypotheses guided the analysis. Comparable worth was more likely to appear in states that were more affluent and were considered to be more innovative or progressive in their adoption of social policies; that generally had a history of support for women's issues; and that probably were unionized and more likely to have "reformed" administrations in both the legislative and executive branches. Factors such as representation of women in the state legislature or economic variables related to working women, such as percentage females in the work force were not ruled out, but experience and the research of others on legislative decision making suggested that these latter factors would be less tangible considerations in the issue's diffusion.[42]

For analysis, the states were divided into four general categories as shown in Figure 4.1 and listed in Table 4.1: comparable worth statute adopters, statute nonadopters, comparable worth study adopters and study nonadopters.

Figure 4.1 Diffusion of Comparable Worth

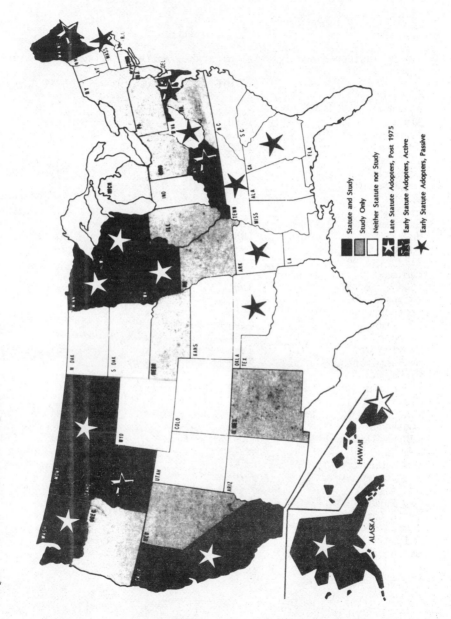

Statute and Study

Study Only

Neither Statute nor Study

Late Statute Adopters, Post 1975

Early Statute Adopters, Active

Early Statute Adopters, Passive

Table 4.1

Incidence and Type of Comparable Worth Activity in the States

	STATUTE	STUDY	1984 ACTION
Alabama	-	-	
Alaska	1980	x	
Arizona	-	-	
Arkansas	1955	-	
California	1981	x	
Colorado	-	-	Failed 1984
Connecticut	-	x	
Delaware	-	-	Passed 1984
Florida	-	-	Failed 1984
Georgia	1966	-	
Hawaii	1982	x	Passed 1984
Idaho	1969	x	
Illinois	-	x	
Indiana	-	-	
Iowa	1984	x	Passed 1984
Kansas	-	-	
Kentucky	1966	x	
Louisiana	-	-	
Maine	1965	x	
Maryland	1966	x	Failed 1984
Massachusetts	1951	-	
Michigan	-	x	
Minnesota	1982	x	
Mississippi	-	-	
Missouri	-	x	Failed 1984
Montana	1983	x	
Nebraska	-	x	Failed 1984
Nevada	-	x	
New Hampshire	-	-	
New Jersey	-	x	
New Mexico	-	x	
New York	-	x	
North Carolina	-	-	
North Dakota	1975	-	
Ohio	-	x	
Oklahoma	1965	-	
Oregon	-	x	
Pennsylvania	-	-	

Table 4.1 (Continued)

Incidence and Type of Comparable Worth Activity in the States

	STATUTE	STUDY	1984 ACTION
Rhode Island	-	-	Passed 1984
South Carolina	-	-	
South Dakota	1978	-	
Tennessee	1974	-	
Texas	-	-	
Utah	-	-	
Vermont	-	-	Passed 1984
Virginia	-	x	Passed 1984
Washington	1983	x	Passed 1984
West Virginia	1965	-	
Wisconsin	1977	x	Passed 1984
Wyoming	-	-	

Date indicates year of passage of statute.
x indicates that a study has been authorized.
- indicates no statute or study.
1984 ACTION column indicates Legislative outcomes of study proposals.

The first category comprises states using comparable worth language in statutes prohibiting discrimination in wages for work done by women; the second, states not employing such language; the third, states that have comparable worth statutes and subsequently have undertaken job evaluation studies; and the fourth, states that have undertaken studies but have no statutes explicitly referencing comparable worth as a standard for prohibiting pay differentials for reasons of sex, or as an evaluation and wage-setting policy.

This section describes states with statutes and those with studies, and the permutations of both that have arisen over the past thirty years. Ten states make up the first subcategory, "early adopters": Arkansas, Georgia, Idaho, Kentucky, Maine, Maryland, Massachusetts, Oklahoma, Tennessee, and West Virginia. They enacted antidiscrimination statutes or incorporated "work of comparable character" language into their fair employment statutes before 1975. Ten other states constitute the subcategory "late adopters": Alaska, California, Hawaii, Iowa, Minnesota, Montana, North Dakota, South Dakota, Washington, and Wisconsin. They used similar statutory language after 1975.

Early statute adopters are further subdivided into states that did nothing more statutorily, "early adopters--passive" (Arkansas, Georgia, Massachusetts, Oklahoma, Tennessee, and West Virginia) and states that had statutory provisions before 1975 and additionally instituted job evaluation studies to assess the presence of wage differentials by sex, "early adopters--active" (Idaho, Kentucky, Maine, and Maryland).

So there is a general pattern of statute adoption. Six states incorporated the language of comparable work or character into antidiscrimination laws before 1975 but took no further action. Four states also enacted such laws before 1975, but went further by putting the concept into practice through policies authorizing job evaluation studies. With the exception of North and South Dakota, all late-adopting states, that is those using comparable worth language in statutes enacted since 1975, went on to authorize studies.

Comparable worth has not been diffused only by statutes prohibiting discrimination. Some states have instituted job evaluation studies and have issued comprehensive statements concerning its use in personnel policy. Of the twenty-five states that currently have completed or are conducting job evaluation studies, roughly half have legislation specifically referencing comparable worth as a standard of evaluation and compensation: Alaska, California, Hawaii, Idaho, Iowa, Kentucky, Maine, Maryland, Minnesota, Montana, Wisconsin, and Washington. Thirteen states have initiated studies without sanctioning comparable worth as a standard: Connecticut, Illinois, Michigan, Missouri, Nebraska, Nevada, New Jersey, New Mexico, New York, Ohio, Oregon, Pennsylvania, and Virginia. It is here argued that the twelve states possessing legislative policy sanctions and completed studies are comparable worth states; all others are not. It is likely that the states that have undertaken studies since 1975 may become comparable worth states, but absent specific legislation sanctioning such a wage and evaluation standard, their status remains subject to administrative discretion and negotiation.[43]

The year 1975 was used to divide the class of statute adopters based on compelling evidence that the diffusion prior to 1975 cannot be imputed with certainty to any singular event or cause. A short review of the characteristics of the early statute adopting--passive

states will show that they are not now, nor were they at
the time of passage of their statutes a part of the
current pay equity movement. Further, they may have
structural, political, or cultural impediments to ever
being so characterized. A look at the timing of the
diffusion in the early adopting--passive states of
Arkansas, Georgia, Massachusetts, Oklahoma, Tennessee,
and West Virginia follows.

Comparable Worth Statute:
Early Adopters--Passive

Arkansas passed its comparable worth statute in 1955
during the administration of Governor Orval E. Faubus.
The state has had liberal to moderate governors, but
Faubus was not one of them. Arkansas has an old-style
southern legislature dominated by white conservative
leaders. It seems unlikely that a state with no
commission on the status on women, that did not ratify
the ERA, that has no provision for collective bargaining
with the state employees, and that has made no job
evaluation studies using comparable worth factors could
be considered an early proponent of comparable worth.[44]
Similarly, Georgia, which adopted a statute with
comparable worth language in 1966, has no commission on
the status of women nor are its state workers unionized,
and it voted no on the ERA ratification in a particularly
fractious battle.[45]

Massachusetts is generally thought to be quite
innovative, but its acceptance of antidiscriminatory
language in 1951 and its strengthening of the statute in
1980 do not make it a comparable worth state. In a
comprehensive sense, it is indisposed to movement on
women's policy concerns. The commission on the status of
women was established in the early 1960s as an
independent entity, not an "ongoing agency of state
government."[46] It has not been strong politically nor has
it followed a consistent advocacy role. Its history has
been punctuated by conflict. Governor King abolished the
commission in 1982, appointing a commission of his own
devising.[47] Members of the former commission went "into
exile," critiquing policy as outsiders.

Massachusetts has fewer women in its legislature
than could be predicted by chance.[48] This anomaly,
shared by Rhode Island, is attributed to a strong
Democratic party dominated by ethnic working-class
members. Diamond speculates that the party's traditional
values have inhibited the recruitment to and
participation of women in elective officeholding.

The state's clerical unions are quiescent. Unions in Massachusetts have declined in membership in the past decade by more than 12 percent. Cook reports that in the public sector AFSCME shows no interest in comparable worth on the state level except at the state colleges.[49]

Of the three remaining early adopter--passive states, Oklahoma, Tennessee, and West Virgina, only West Virginia had a history of strong labor ties and some liberal traditions. Elazar reports that although no southern states, regardless of how urbanized, had antidiscrimination legislation in 1961, border states Kentucky and West Virginia had established human relations commissions.[50] Passage of the ERA in West Virginia is attributed more to the control of the Senate by liberal Democrats than to consensus in the state over women's issues.[51] West Virginia has unions in the public sector but they may not bargain over wages--a condition shared by unions in Washington and several other states.[52]

Oklahoma and Tennessee are classified as early adopters--passive because of their lack of any subsequent comparable worth activity. Oklahoma is a noncompetitive state politically in its party alignment. It does not have collective bargaining for state employees, and did not ratify the Equal Rights Amendment. It does have a commission on the status of women, but no money is appropriated to it.[53]

Tennessee is dominated by single-party, Democratic politics, has no collective bargaining in the public sector at the state level, rescinded its ratification of the ERA, and abolished its commission on the status of women. Comparable worth statutory language was passed during a time of power shifts in state government when Governor Ray Blanton was "convicted of selling gubernatorial pardons."[54]

Those states labeled early adopters--passive have remained just outside the mainstream of the pay equity movement up to the present. Tennessee enacted a classification study effective 1 July 1984, but it does not have explicit comparable worth policy statements attached. Massachusetts considered but failed to pass a comparable worth study resolution in 1982.

Comparable Worth Statute:
Early Adopters--Active

The states designated early adopters--active are unusual for a number of reasons. Idaho, Kentucky, Maine, and Maryland illustrate the great diversity of characteristics that draw comparable worth together as an issue. Idaho is considered a comparable worth state. It represents comparable worth's use as a management issue rather than as a women's, labor, or personnel policy issue. Like Tennessee and West Virginia, it is marked by strong urban-rural ideological splits. Although a two-party competitive state, its governor is most often a Republican. Its conservative and liberal Republican legislators are balanced by the preponderance of moderates in committee leadership positions. Remick credits Idaho with enacting comparable worth "without mentioning sex equity."[55] It abolished its commission on the status of women, rescinded its vote ratifying the ERA, and does not allow collective bargaining for state employees. Legislation in 1975 required a job classification study that was implemented in 1977. Salaries for female-dominated occupations were adjusted upward in amounts reportedly running between 10 to 30 percent.[56] The work force of 8,400 is tiny compared to the national average, thus offering insights into why management could do so well, absent well-organized interests with independent power resources.

Kentucky is like Idaho in one regard: it, too, rescinded ratification of the ERA. Its job evaluation study was set in motion by a Senate resolution in July 1982. The state's work force is not unionized, and is considered a two-party competitive state. Kentucky state government in the 1960s was conservative in economics and in civil rights.[57] Comparable worth legislation was passed in 1966. Many women have run for governor, and the current governor, Martha Layne Collins, had the support of Wendell Ford, a former governor. Ford is noted for his "turning point" election in 1971, won through the support of labor and teacher groups.[58] Kentucky's commission on the status of women has one of the largest commission budgets in the country.

Maine also is a two-party competitive state, its employees are unionized, it has a commission on the status of women, and it was an early ratifier of the ERA. The comparable worth statute, passed in 1965, lay dormant until a review of Maine's classification and compensation system in 1975. Controversy and grievances surrounded the study. In 1979 the Maine State Employees Association (MSEA) introduced comparable worth into collective bargaining, agreeing to a to a $100,000 study in 1982.

Maryland, the last state in this category, adopted comparable worth language prohibiting discrimination in 1966, as had Kentucky and Georgia. Maryland is a one-party noncompetitive state where Democrats "preside over a landslide election every four years."[59] A 1979 study commission's report on the state government compensation system was criticized for not seeming to concern itself with potential undervaluation of work performed predominantly by women. A second study was authorized and requests for proposals were sought in the spring of 1984. Maryland was an early ratifier of the ERA, has a very active commission on women, and has unionized employees. Additionally, organized labor is considered a powerful interest group, particularly the AFL-CIO and the Maryland Classified Employees Association.[60]

In summary, although ten states had comparable worth language in statutes prohibiting discrimination enacted before 1975, only four were seemingly caught up in the later pay equity movement's scrutiny of classification and pay plans for inequities due to sex. North and South Dakota passed legislation in 1975 and 1978 but did no more, and should probably be set within the early adopter--passive category, irrespective of date of passage. Populism was once the hallmark of both Dakotas, but today there is business-oriented Republicanism in the North Dakota Senate and governorship and conservative Republicanism in the South Dakota legislature and governorship.[61]

Four of the early-adopting states went on to commission studies, and all but two of the late-adopting states did likewise. The remainder of the chapter juxtaposes the set of twelve states adopting studies that have comparable worth legislation (referred to below as statute states) and the set of thirteen states initiating studies that do not have comparable worth legislation (referred to as study states).

The States Authorizing Studies: With Comparable Worth Statutes and Without

What social, political, or economic factors accounted for the formal commitment of the resources of twenty-five states to the study of comparable worth? Are there differences between factors found in states adopting statutes and studies after 1975, and those states adopting only studies?

Theory provides a number of factors that should be thought about. First is whether comparable worth represented simply another interest group coup, that is,

that one could predict that the higher the level of
unionization, the more the institutionalization of
women's issues--such as acceptance of the ERA or
commission on status of women agencies. Or, the greater
the proportion of women in the legislature, the greater
the probability of acceptance of comparable worth.
Alternatively, it might be argued that interest group
activity is incidental to the appearance and serious
consideration of comparable worth; that the diffusion of
comparable worth is a product of the cultural and
political nuances of each state. Perhaps the cultural
factors identified by Elazar of Traditionalism, Moralism,
and Individualism--characteristics of states that govern
political intervention in bureaucratic affairs--are
operative here. States that are designated Moralist may
see intervention of this type as being for the good of
the community; states designated Individualistic may see
comparable worth as improving the efficient use of
government resources; and states described as
Traditionalist may oppose government programs to expand
bureaucratic attachments and enhancements.

Equally as arguable might be subsets of the
diffusion of innovation themes: that programs to
rationalize classification and pay plans would fall more
readily into policy initiatives of the "pioneer states"
identified by Walker as states that are wealthier, better
staffed, or professionalized and opportunistic in their
scanning of potential policies and programs.
"Innovators" are states that adopt or set trends of
statute adoption more rapidly than other states.

Because of the specialized nature of job evaluation
and analysis, and the monopoly personnel specialists
exert over both, it seems reasonable to consider, too,
whether the civil service reform that brought
governmental reorganization of administrative services
might possibly have had a measurable effect on the
diffusion of comparable worth as well.

Finally, economic variables. Some are peculiar to
comparable worth as a women's issue, such as the
percentage of women in the work force of the state.
Other more speculative factors, such as the level of debt
per capita, shed light on a possible relationship between
a state's deficit spending and its proclivity to enact or
postpone pay changes for its employees.

Table 4.2

Comparison of the Correlates of Policy Choices in
Comparable Worth: Statute States or Study States

INDEPENDENT VARIABLES	STATUTE STATES (N=12)	STUDY STATES (N=13)
Administrative Variables		
--Reorganization--Civil Service Administration	.19	.18
--Legislative Professionalism	.01	.43
Political Variables		
--Innovativeness	.25	.40
--Political Culture	-.30	-.31
--Governor's Power	.09	.43
--Party Competitiveness	-.20	-.34
Women's Political Variables		
--Equal Rights Amendment	.28	.20
--Commissions on the Status of Women	-.06	.14
--Number of Women Legislators	-.02	-.02
Socioeconomic Variables		
--Unionization	-.20	.42
--Per Capita Income	.12	.40
--Pay of State Employees	-.01	.28
--State Debt	.24	.15
--Percentage of Women Employed in Work Force	.26	.04

The twelve Study states having comparable worth legislation are Alaska, California, Hawaii, Idaho, Iowa, Kentucky, Maine, Maryland, Minnesota, Montana, Washington, and Wisconsin. The thirteen states having only studies are Connecticut, Illinois, Michigan, Missouri, Nebraska, Nevada, New Jersey, New Mexico, New York, Ohio, Oregon, Pennsylvania (university-sponsored study), and Virginia.

Sources of the Independent Variable Measures

1. Reorganization: Civil Service Reform Activity in the States, Index devised by D. Dresang, "Diffusion of Civil Service Reform: State and Local

Government," Review of Public Personnel Administration 2 (Spring 1982), Table 1, pp. 38-39.

2. Legislative Professionalism: Index in S.M. Morehouse, State Politics, Parties, and Policy (New York: Holt, Rinehart and Winston, 1980), Appendix Eight, pp. 513-14.

3. Innovativeness: Index of R.L. Savage, "Policy Innovativeness as a Trait of American States," Journal of Politics 40 (1978), p. 216.

4. Political Culture: Ira Sharkansky's Index constructed from Elazar's political culture theory, in "The Utility of Elazar's Political Culture: A Research Note," Polity 2 (Fall 1969), p. 72.

5. Governor's Power: Index of Formal Power of the Governor by Joseph Schlesinger, reproduced in Morehouse, State Politics, Parties, and Policy, Appendix Two, pp. 493-94.

6. Party Competitiveness: "Measures of Party Competition for States, 1961-1982," in M.E. Jewell and D.M. Olson, American State Political Parties and Elections (Homewood, IL: Dorsey Press, 1982), Table 2.1, p. 27.

7. Equal Rights Amendment: "Typology of State Responses to the ERA, 1972-1978," in J.K. Boles, The Politics of the Equal Rights Amendment (New York: Longman, 1979), p. 22.

8. Commissions on the Status of Women: Directory provided by the Women's Bureau, Washington, DC, 1983.

9. Number of Women Legislators: National Directory of Women Elected Officials (Washington, DC: National Women's Political Caucus, 1982), pp. 6-9.

10. Unionization: "State Employee Labor Relations: Public Unions," Council of State Governments, Book of the States, 1982-1983 (Lexington, KY: CSG, 1983).

11. Per Capita Income: "Personal Income Per Capita," U.S. Dept. of Commerce, Bureau of the Census, Statistical Abstract, 1982-83 (Washington, DC: Government Printing Office, 1982).

12. Pay of State Employees: "State and Local Government Payrolls and Average Earnings of Full-Time Employees, by State," Book of the States, 1981-82, p. 342.

13. State Debt: "State and Local Governments--Debt Outstanding by States: 1975 to 1980," U.S. Department of Commerce, Bureau of the Census, Statistical Abstract of the United States (Washington, DC: Government Printing Office, 1983), p. 286.

14. Percentage of Women Employed in State Work Force: "Characteristics of the Civilian Labor Force, by State: 1981," Statistical Abstract of the United States (1983), p. 378.

Table 4.2 shows Pearson-product-moment correlation coefficients for the independent variables and the two policy choices: having a statute and a study, on the one hand, or having only a study. The first category is labeled statute states in the table, the second category is labeled study states. Three factors are important for their association with studies: legislative professionalism, governor's power, and unionization, with innovativeness and per capita income close behind. For the statute-adopting states having studies, only one of these factors, innovativeness, plays a role. Associations in the statute-adopting states are with such factors as ERA ratification, percentage of women in the work force, and state debt. Unionization is negatively associated in this instance with statute-adopting states. Elazar's categorical regions based on political culture are also negatively associated with statute-adopting states.

What do these findings suggest? First, that there is some support for the idea that study adoption is more highly associated with factors of innovativeness, political and administrative sophistication, unionization, and wealth. And, that study-adopting states are different from statute-adopting states in regard to a number of political and economic factors. Chapter 5 assays the importance of these statistical inferences for predicting implementation, or enhancing our knowledge of possible future political consensus on comparable worth.

NOTES

1. C. B. Ransone, Jr., The American Governorship (Westport, CT, 1982), p. 43.
2. H. Remick, "Beyond Equal Pay for Equal Work: Comparable Worth in the State of Washington," in Equal Employment Policy for Women, ed. R. Steinberg Ratner (Philadelphia, 1980), p. 408.
3. Although it is not known how many women in the general population subscribe to the view that states are innovative, judging from the constitutions and practices of such traditional women's groups long active in state politics as the League of Women Voters (LWV) and the American Association of University Women (AAUW), the author deems reasonable the generalization that such

groups perceive the states to be innovative and to be receptive testing grounds for new policies. Care should be exercised in generalizing this to the entire population of women. Research on political attitudes and behavior of women suggests that men and women have different orientations in general political interest, or interest in a particular level of government. Also there are differences in attention of women to politics via media usage, and participation in politics. Jennings and Niemi find that in comparison with men, women generally insulate themselves from the political process, are not as interested in political affairs, nor do they read about, listen to, or attend to political matters as much as do men. Further, women interested in politics attend more to state and local than national or international affairs. M.K. Jennings and R.G. Niemi, Generations and Politics (Princeton, NJ, 1981), pp. 275-83. See also R. L. Savage, "Policy Innovativeness as a Trait of American States," Journal of Politics 40 (1978), p. 219.

4. J.A. Grune, ed., Manual on Pay Equity (Washington, DC, 1980), p. 117.

5. M.K. Jennings and H. Zeigler, "The Salience of American State Politics," in State and Urban Politics, ed. R.I. Hofferbert and I. Sharkansky (Boston, 1971).

6. Conclusions of S.M. Morehouse, State Politics, Parties and Policy (New York, 1980), pp. 10-11; and J.D. Nowlan, The Politics of Higher Education (Urbana, 1976). For discussion of how the majority of states handled conflict of interest and election laws, see H. Alexander, Campaign Money (New York, 1976).

7. See the "Law of Participants' Perspectives" in D. Wright, Understanding Intergovernmental Relations, (North Scituate, MA, 1978), pp. 75-76, for discussion of perspectives of federal, state, and local officers toward the other levels of government: the upper level sees an inverted pyramid, with expansive judgment flowing from the top, and narrow parochialism at the bottom; state officers see a diamond form of judgment exhibited, with their level as the widest, most expansive, and most potent; and local officers see an hour-glass configuration, with broadness of judgment at the national and local levels, and a bottleneck of narrow parochialism at the state level.

8. F. Barbash, "State Courts Emerge as Protectors of Individual Rights," Washington Post National Weekly, 16 April 1984; and R. L. Stanfield, "All the Way to the Supreme Court: States Make Federalism a Federal Case," National Journal, 14 January 1984, pp. 71-74, are two articles out of literally dozens that point to a new activism and engagement in a wide array of moral, social, and political issues emanating from the states.

9. Wright, Understanding Intergovernmental Relations, p. 253. C. W. Steinberg, "Beyond the Days of

Wine and Roses," Public Administration Review 41
(January-February 1981), pp. 10-11, reviews the dollar
growth in federal aid to state and local governments as
having "climbed from approximately $7 billion in FY 1960
to an estimated $88.9 billion in FY 1980." Instruments
for aid dispersal have become more numerous and diverse.
Of special concern to Steinberg is the phenomenon of
bypassing. He writes: "The jurisdictional 'leapfrogging'
tendencies of federal agencies and congressional
committees have become more pronounced. They have
created difficulties in subnational planning,
coordination, and implementation activities. States in
particular have been affected. They have been bypassed
in the administration of approximately 25 percent of
federal assistance, even though many have assumed key
roles in the same program areas...that are being handled
on a federal-local basis." Steinberg echoes the warning
offered a dozen years ago by Daniel Elazar in "The
American Partnership: The Next Half Generation," The
Politics of American Federalism, ed. D. Elazar (Boston,
1969), pp. 221-25. He writes that "states will have to
act with greater vigor to maintain their traditional
positions as the keystones of the American governmental
arch. The significance of the states will depend on
their ability to respond to the challenges of direct
federal-local aid. States will have to initiate their
own programs to deal with local problems rather than
merely act as conduits funneling federal aid to local
communities and local requests to Washington."

10. Ibid., p. 285.
11. Ibid.
12. For a historical and analytic discussion of the
role of "legislative professionalism," see J.G. Grumm,
"The Effects of Legislative Structure on Legislative
Performance," in State and Urban Politics, ed. R.I.
Hofferbert and I. Sharkansky (Boston, 1971), pp. 298-322.
R. Huwa and A. Rosenthal, Politicians and Professionals
(New Brunswick, NJ, 1977), p. 1, report the "staff
capacity of legislative committees has grown notably.
Data from forty states for the period 1968 to 1974
indicate an increase of about 600 percent in committee
staffing, from 65 to 495 professionals."
13. Wright, Understanding Intergovernmental
Relations, p. 285. See also "Power Shifts in State
Capitols as Professional Lawmakers Take Over Leadership
Spots," Congressional Quarterly, 3 September 1983, pp.
1767-69.
14. R. Sherrill, "Florida's Legislature: The Pork
Chop State of Mind," Harper's, November 1965, pp. 82-97,
describes the prereapportionment domination of the
legislature by a "little clique of back country
Senators--relics from a smug, sleepy, past," who disliked
being thought of "as a gang which would go in and rape

the treasury." Sherrill thought them so conservative in
their philosophy and voting habits that "the treasury is
seldom full enough to make the trip worthwhile." Swift
to appropriate millions for highway construction, and for
screwworm, burrowing nematode, and fire ant eradication
(enemies of the cow, the orange, and the farmer), the
pork-chop legislators grudgingly passed aid for dependent
children of $86 a month in 1965, $4 more than in 1955,
and roundly defeated bids by the governor for a consumer
watchdog agency.

Sherrill characterized the government as not ugly
but rather "rickety," like many state governments of the
time. Florida had no corporate income tax or state
property tax, and made few demands on the paper mills,
insurance companies, banks, mines, and timber companies.
Its "billion dollar citrus industry /paid/ almost no tax,
and those it /did/ pay /were/ specifically earmarked to
be spent in advertising and promoting citrus." Before
reapportionment, the pork-chop patriarchs of the Senate
came from districts with typically ten to twenty thousand
people; senators from Dade County represented one million
constituents.

15. D.R. Colburn and R.K. Scher, Florida's
Gubernatorial Poltics in the 20th Century/ (Tallahassee,
1980), p. 31.

16. Nowland, The Politics of Higher Education, p.
vii.

17. See synopsis of Baker v. Carr and Reynolds v.
Sims in Morehouse, Politics, Parties and Policy, pp.
265-66.

18. A. Rosenthal, The Improvement of State
Legislatures--The First Five Years of Eagleton's
Legislative Center (New Brunswick, NJ, October 1971).

19. Huwa and Rosenthal, Politicians and
Professionals, p. 1.

20. L. Sabato, "Governor's Office Careers: A New
Breed Emerges," State Government, Summer 1979, pp.
95-102.

21. Morehouse, Politics, Parties and Policy, pp.
132-33.

22. L. Sabato, Goodbye to Goodtime Charlie: The
American Governor Transformed, 1950-1975 (Lexington, MA,
1978).

23. See survey of state agency heads conducted by
Wright, in Wright, Understanding Intergovernmental
Relations, p. 246.

24. Ibid. Wright reports women agency heads were
only 2 percent in 1964, and 8 percent in 1978.

25. The number of women legislators doubled in
approximately the same time span. Ransone, The American
Governorship, p. 42, reports that the 101 women senators
and 601 women representatives in 1977 were more than

double those serving a decade before. M.K. Hedblom,
Women and Political Organizations and Institutions
(Washington, DC, 1984), p. 42, reports that in 1969 women
held 6 percent of the seats in state legislatures; in
1978, 9 percent; and in 1981, 12 percent. Few formal
surveys of the representativeness of women in the levels
below agency head exist. Ransone informally notes in his
two surveys of governor's offices that the changes
between 1956 and 1976 were dramatic. There were no women
employed in principal staff assistant slots in the early
study; later he found that often "the governor's
principal assistant, press secretary, or principal
legislative liaison officers were women" (p. 42).
  26. Wright, _Understanding Intergovernmental
Relations_, p. 246.
  27. Ibid.
  28. Huwa and Rosenthal, _Politicians and
Professionals_, p. 8.
  29. N. Peirce, "State-Local Report/ Structural
Reform of Bureaucracy Grows Rapidly," _National Journal_,
15 April 1975, pp. 502-8, found twenty states had
undergone substantial reorganization since 1965, and
twenty more had achieved partial reorganization by
consolidating departments. D. L. Dresang, "Diffusion of
Civil Service Reform: The Federal and State Governments,"
Review of Public Personnel Administration 2 (Spring
1982), pp. 35-47, notes twenty-four states with
reorganization activities. D.M. Fox, "Reorganizing State
Government," _The Bureaucrat_ 10 (Fall 1981), pp. 69-70,
notes twenty-three states.
  30. See review of the literature profiling the
separate research foci used in political science in H.
Jacob and M. Lipsky, "Outputs, Structure and Power: An
Assessment of the Changes in the Study of State and Local
Politics," in _State and Urban Politics_, ed. R.I.
Hofferbert and I. Sharkansky (Boston, 1971). For an
update on the status of the literature see L.P. Stavisky,
"State Legislatures and the New Federalism," _Public
Administration Review_ 41 (November-December 1981), pp.
701-10.
  31. Alexander, _Campaign Money_.
  32. Wright, _Understanding Intergovernmental
Relations_, p. 247.
  33. See excellent discussion of changes in
requirements and funding in Wright, _Understanding
Intergovernmental Relations_, and an outline of the Reagan
administration's plans for revamping the federal
grant-and-aid system to transfer programs and taxing
responsibilities to the states in N. Peirce, "New Panels
to Move Quickly to Help Reagan 'Unbend' the Federal
System," _National Journal_, 2 May 1981, pp. 785-88; D.B.
Walker, _Toward a Functioning Federalism_ (Cambridge, MA,
1981); and the three-year, eleven-volume study of the

Advisory Commission on Intergovernmental Relations, The
Federal Role in the Federal System: The Dynamic of
Growth, 1980-1981, point to a narrowing policy space for
the states because of an overload of responsibilities and
mandatory cutbacks in services due to lack of revenue.

34. G.B. Merry, "Citizen-Initiated Legislation May
Be on the Ballot in 19 States," Christian Science
Monitor, 15 May 1984, p. 7.

35. See chapter 3 on pressure groups in the states
in Morehouse, Politics, Parties and Policy, pp. 95-142;
also see discussion of post-reapportionment power status
in Colburn and Scher, Florida's Gubernatorial Politics in
the Twentieth Century, p. 31.

36. J.L. Walker, "The Diffusion of Innovations among
the Several States," American Political Science Review 63
(1969), pp. 880-99; V. Gray, "Innovation in the States: A
Diffusion Study," American Political Science Review 67
(December 1973), pp. 1174-86; S. Welch and K. Thompson,
"The Impact of Federal Incentives on State Policy
Innovation," American Journal of Political Science 24
(November 1980), pp. 715-29; M. Daniels and R. Darcy, "As
Time Goes By: The Arrested Diffusion of the Equal Rights
Amendment," Publius (forthcoming, 1984); R. Eyestone,
"Confusion, Diffusion, and Innovation," American
Political Science Review 71 (June 1977), pp. 441-47; R.L.
Savage, "Policy Innovativeness as a Trait of American
States," The Journal of Politics 40 (1978), pp. 212-24;
J.L. Walker, "Comment: Problems in Research on the
Diffusion of Policy Innovations," American Political
Science Review 67 (December 1973), pp. 1186-91; and V.
Gray, "Rejoinder to 'Comment' by J.D. Walker," American
Political Science Review 67 (December 1973), pp. 1192-93.

37. For a cogent description of J. Schlesinger's
Index of Competition, see Morehouse, State Politics,
Parties and Policy, p. 66.

38. Gray, "Innovation in the States," p. 1183.

39. Ibid., p. 1176.

40. Walker, "Comment," p. 1187.

41. Gray, "Innovation in the States," p. 1184.

42. I. Diamond, Sex Roles in the Legislature (New
Haven, 1977).

43. New Mexico is an exception. It has completed a
study and implemented it. But the examples of multiple
deterrents to implementation are more numerous in this
second set of states. The most famous, Washington,
adopted comparable worth legislation in the wake of
deliberation about its $1 billion court case. For a
detailed account of the debate in the House and Senate
during the 1983 session over increasing or only adjusting
women's salaries, see H. Remick, "An Update on Washington
State," Public Personnel Management 14 (Winter 1983), pp.
390-94. In contrast, Connecticut has received very
little attention during its five years of studies brought

forth by three separate pieces of legislation, none of
which creates explicit policy sanctions for comparability
standards. Study findings will be subject to negotiation
through collective bargaining, and are intensively
monitored because of the $300 million district court
suit. See A.H. Cook, Comparable Worth (Manoa, HI, 1983),
p. 37.

44. "Profiles of the 50 States," Congressional
Quarterly, 3 September 1983, pp. 1777-78; and M. Barone
and G. Ujifusa, The Almanac of American Politics
(Washington, DC, 1984), pp. 53-68. Generally references
to unionization of a state's work force do not include
teacher, municipal, public safety, or fire unions, which
are often exceptions in collective bargaining laws.

45. J.K. Boles, The Politics of the Equal Rights
Amendment (New York, 1979), devotes a lengthy
consideration to Georgia gender politics.

46. Women's Bureau, Statutory Commissions on the
Status of Women (a background report)(Washington, DC,
1969).

47. Cook, Comparable Worth, p. 37.

48. Diamond, Sex Roles in the Legislature, pp.
17-20.

49. U.S. Department of Commerce, Bureau of the
Census, "Labor Organization Membership 1970-1980,"
Statistical Abstract (Washington, DC, 1983), Table 682,
p. 409. The health and status of the dominant clerical
union in a state does play a strong role in how the issue
will develop. AFSCME-Florida was forestalling bankruptcy
during its last negotiations, a contingency destined to
weaken its legislative effectiveness. Similarly,
AFSCME's clerical unions in other states, such as
Michigan and Connecticut, were organized late and are not
considered as strong as other longer-established state
unions.

50. D. Elazar, American Federalism: A View from the
States (New York, 1960), p. 150.

51. "Profiles of the 50 States," pp. 1866-67.

52. Council on State Governments, Book of the
States, 1980-1981 (Lexington, KY, 1982), p. 345. State
Representative Shelby Leary reported to the Conference
for Women State Legislators, 2-3 December 1983, San
Diego, California, sponsored by the Carnegie Foundation,
that "West Virginia is so far behind /it/ just passed a
civil service bill covering many of those state employees
who . . . make wages so low that they can receive food
stamps and welfare." (Taped remarks transcribed by the
author.)

53. Women's Bureau, Commissions for Women: Moving in
the 1980s (Washington, DC, 1980).

54. Barone and Ujifusa, Almanac of American
Politics, p. 1092.

55. Remick, "Beyond Equal Pay for Equal Work," pp.

405-18.

56. Cook, *Comparable Worth*, p. 73.
57. Barone and Ujifusa, *Almanac of American Politics*, p. 448.
58. Ibid.
59. "Profile of the 50 States," pp. 1810-11.
60. Ibid.
61. Ibid., pp. 1838-39 and 1852-53.

5
What Changes Are Sought?

INTRODUCTION

Each of the states described in Chapter 4 responded to the introduction of comparable worth in its own unique way. The diffusion pattern itself confirms that the innovativeness of the states--their propensity to experiment with and adopt new legislation--did play a major role in adoptions of comparable worth studies since 1975. But what of implementation? Do the states respond, administratively, in the same manner? Were the changes sought in all of the states uniform? What accounts for the smooth transition of some states and apparent lack of controversy, and the consternation and tortured route to implementation of others? What political, social, or administrative factors account for the differences among implementation products in the states? Hargrove offers good advice in regard to assessing implementation.

If programs have multiple and conflicting goals because of the nature of politics in a democratic society, how does one judge implementation a success or failure? ... The first answer is that /one/ accepts the fact of multiple goals and seeks to explain the factors that facilitate and hinder the attainment of each. The very facts of normative ambiguity and complexity and the existence of contradictory strategies within the same program are the subject of implementation research.... /The/ purpose is to be able to say in an objective way that strategy X will likely achieve consequences Y with implications for goal Z.[1]

An authoritatively adopted policy, then, is usually "only a collection of words prior to implementation. At most it is a point of departure for bargaining among implementers."[2]

This chapter looks at the circumstances surrounding implementation that have produced different strategies and products. It queries whether those charged with implementation play a role in defining an optimum strategy for implementation, or whether personnel directors only mirror the degree of consensus they find in their states at any time on any given issue.

Background. The general political climate in which states operated in the period from the late 1970s to the early 1980s was one of flux. The Democratic party recaptured thirty to thirty-five of the governorships in the wake of Watergate, reversing the party dominance that Republican governors had enjoyed during the late Vietnam era.[3] Dresang reports that the civil service reform activity in reorganization from 1975 to 1977 of more than thirty-three states leveled off in 1978-80 to only eleven additional states. Many more state personnel agencies tried lesser innovations in the later period, such as in performance evaluation, whistle-blowing laws, and senior executive service rather than in structural or functional reorganization.[4]

What was more widely shared as a multistate phenomenon in the early 1980s were expressions at professional conferences, in the press, and in surveys of administrators that there was "quantum change" afoot, and that uncertainty dominated decision making, as did lack of planning and management analysis. This was particularly evident in personnel management, where initiatives of the Reagan administration directed toward reducing the scope of government at all levels by narrowing programs and program size had their first effect.[5] Personnel agencies became the front line in conflict over the scope of government and planned change.

Interest groups within government and outside it "discovered" personnel in the late 1970s and early 1980s, and attempted to master its labyrinth of technical and ideological mechanisms. The scrutiny raised new questions: Had personnel been unfairly characterized as the Rip Van Winkle of government--garbed in unending forms and uttering archaic hyperbole about the dangers of politics--while becoming more politicized? Was it an unfair impression that its directors only "hovered in the administrative shadows assuming housekeeping roles in the authority networks" where the real decisions were made?[6] To gain some perspective on how the speed and level of demands for change impacted personnel at large during

this time, it is necessary to know something about its
theoretical and practical underpinnings as an
administrative function in government.

PERSONNEL AS EXECUTIVE FUNCTION

The director of management development and research
for the Council of State Governments wrote in 1982 that
just the short period 1980-82 constituted "an era" in
development of state personnel systems. His litany of
reasons for his characterization included funding
reductions, deletion of federal support, cutback
management, comparative pay, productivity, and
unionization, as well as abolition of the merit system.[7]
These elements constitute some of the problems of
personnel management, but there are others more systemic
and long standing. One major problem for personnel
managers in the states has been to discover how to
"attenuate the impact of political debate" and conflict
among institutional actors so that some acceptable level
of professional service might be performed.[8] Public
personnel has traditionally sought solutions in the form
of organizational and political remedies.

Organizationally, personnel has refined a large
array of practices to select, develop, and evaluate
people. The practices must meet several conflicting value
premises: the demand for representativeness, political
neutrality, and competence, while maintaining some
semblance of executive responsibility.[9] Variously labeled
"merit systems," "classification plans," and the like,
the practices come in forms that depend on each state's
history, culture, and level of political intervention.

Merit system integration into the personnel
practices of the states is a special case that warrants
analysis. By 1974 thirty-four states had adopted
statewide systems, and sixteen more had partial coverage
along the lines of merit. Further, most large cities had
some merit system, particularly those with populations
over 250,000. Shafritz and others find that this
occurred because of two overriding factors. First,
government responsibility had become so complex that
patronage in many locales had to give way to technical
proficiency. Second, the federal government threw its
weight toward the "development of forceful merit systems
at the state and local levels."[10] The enactment of the
Intergovernmental Personnel Act of 1970 (IPA) exerted a
powerful influence by providing grants to improve state
and local personnel systems through training facilities
for their employees and information exchange.

Welch and Thompson's research on the impact of federal incentives on state policy innovations notes that states stood to lose federal funding if they did not implement a merit personnel system.[11] Such negative incentives insured that the policies would diffuse faster than those initiated by individual states. There have been exceptions to the accelerating effect of federal interest in a policy: civil rights and education policies generally took longer to be accepted irrespective of federal interest or incentive.

Politically, personnel has progressed in most states to the status of an executive agency receiving somewhat limited oversight from other institutions because of the technical nature of its work. This status was the result of events in the 1970s that resulted in organizational changes, or the semblance of changes. The first change was the replacement in many jurisdictions of the commission form of governance with a single director; the second, the use of merit in selection, promotion, and pay. It is not too implausible to think that what may have been diffused in the 1970s, was the "shadow of merit"--its form but not its substance. Because of the speed and direction of change desired by federal sponsors, merit principles did not necessarily accompany the changes in structure in many states. The directors, newly autonomous from the civil service commission, were also detached from gubernatorial control because of the technical complexity of their work. They may only have copied symbolic and cosmetic personnel innovations rather than deal with the equity and redistributive issues coincident with the idea of merit because of the issues' high political cost. This may explain why merit system "reform" diffused so rapidly when equally volatile innovations, such as civil rights and education, were accepted more slowly during the same period.

Theoretically, one can view public personnel "as a complex organizational system rather than primarily a technical or political system."[12] As such it has three levels of responsibility and control: institutional, organizational, and technical. The institutional level consists of those rule-making and enforcement bodies who debate and possess the power to determine questions of the wider purpose of organizations: issues of social legitimacy, value, character, and fiscal and programmatic viability for personnel operations. The organizational level performs intermediary functions, and is essentially dominated by managers who operate in two directions simultaneously: translating debate and "general policy guidance" into "concrete decision premises for the technical core of the organization," then taking the information about technical limitations of potential actions back to the institutional level to refine policy. The technical level does not just passively receive decision premises and routinize work. It tells management how existing technology may or may not be suited to achieving institutional goals. The central rule for organizational viability is that the technical core be protected from uncertainty and political intervention.

The paramount political question for personnel managers in achieving these organizational ends is choosing which set of actors at the institutional level offers the most justifiable criteria for the selection and allocation of personnel, demands the least accountability, and provides the most stable fiscal, programmatic, and political support. Viewed organizationally, personnel has chosen a fairly consistent institutional affiliation, since the 1930s: a management function with a single director "within the executive chain of command."[13] Viewed politically, it is anybody's guess whose music personnel marches to at any one time. Governors come and go. Other agencies, strong pressure groups, and leadership cliques in the legislature have considerable staying and saying power, as do the media. Only intensive reference group and decision-making research would offer any certainty for understanding long-term institutional allegiances in fact. The evidence from a 1984 survey of the fifty state personnel directors by the author on this issue suggests that comparable worth studies are most likely to be found in states with both higher levels of legislative professionalism and greater formal powers for the governor.

MECHANISMS FOR ENACTMENT AND IMPLEMENTATION

There are as many models of enactment of comparable worth as there are states involved, for example, blue-ribbon committees, and oversight advisory committees, some heavily dominated by labor, others by management, still others by legislative appointees. Enactment also has occurred through executive order or collective bargaining, with later appropriations by the legislature as a signal of political viability. Studies have occurred with large consultant services and oversight; others have had large in-house staff involvement and minimal consultancies. All these variations are represented in the twenty-five active states.

Chapter 3 depicted Connecticut proponents' agenda-setting strategies that were linked to plans for implementation. These and other examples show a few of the wide range of activities in the public sector for using comparable worth's evaluation methodologies to ascertain and later to remedy wage disparities. The question of who is advantaged in implementation by what legislative strategies during agenda setting, under what conditions, cannot be answered completely. The most that can be ascertained is whether any model of implementation seems more efficacious than any other, and by what standards this is so. The role of personnel managers during agenda setting is not known, and may not be known until case studies are published.

Managers'atttitudes toward comparable worth, and their impressions of support for it in the general political community are projected from results of the abovementioned survey. Three examples of implementation in the states are discussed below, followed by a summary of the survey. The concluding section draws inferences from the implementation examples and the questionnaire responses.

✓ **Three Examples.** Connecticut, Washington, and Minnesota serve as examples of implementation. Connecticut and Washington have been discussed earlier, and are reviewed here only briefly; new information on Minnesota is introduced. The three states were chosen for their similarities to one another across a number of important characteristics, and their dissimilarities in approaches to implementation. The characteristics that they share are innovativeness, the number of unionized state workers, number of women state legislators, state payroll, and per capita income. All are within the range of political culture Elazar calls Moralistic: Minnesota---moralistic; Washington--moralistic-individualistic; and Connecticut--individualistic-moralistic.[14]

Women in the Washington legislature as recently as December 1983 were still recounting what Remick terms "the harrowing chain of events" during a regular and special session that year when they worked with coalitions of feminist groups and a few unions to put together legislation and funding to implement comparable worth. The women legislators introduced an appropriations bill with a $1.5 million implementation price tag so as to capture the approval of the leadership and insure later passage. Representative Jennifer Belcher told how her colleague Shirley Galloway inserted an amendment at 5 A.M. during one session: "We got it on the floor before anybody realized what was happening, and we had our leadership and the rest of our members in a situation where they would have been embarrassed to vote no."[15] In retrospect, both Belcher and Senator Eleanor Lee emphasized bipartisanship as a key to facilitating passage of bills for implementation. Lee, whose tenure dates from 1974,

offered a prescription for adopting a plan of action to
remedy wage disparities. First, perform a competent job
evaluation; second, require regular updates by law; and
last, have an implementation plan. She then reviewed
what she thought the Washington case offered to other
states.

> While lawyers are arguing and appeals
> are pending a wise legislature will adopt
> a plan of action, and spread it over a
> period of time that will not break the
> budget...in a way that can be administered
> with a reasonably high degree of
> precision, fairness, and certainty. If
> /they/ do not, /they'll/ find themselves
> at the end of a five or more year history
> of appeals with a judgment day disaster,
> pay disparities greater than now exist,
> financial chaos to fulfill a court remedy,
> and the risk of new discrimination and
> inequities in cases of hasty action.[16]

In Minnesota, implementation has been achieved, or
is certainly close. No 5 A.M. appropriations riders to
catch the unwary, no billion-dollar court suit. Senator
Linda Bergman, who has served in the legislature since
1972 and is currently assistant majority leader,
summarized Minnesota's history on the issue. Her highest
priority was "getting the principle of pay equity
established in the law."[17] The lawmakers achieved that
and more.

Minnesota established a job evaluation system under
contract with Hay and Associates in 1979. In 1981 a task
force was created by the legislative advisory Council on
the Economic Status of Women to look at the economic
condition of women in the public sector. Among the major
concerns was the rising feminization of poverty. The
task force was broadly representative, with members from
the House and Senate, Department of Employee Relations,
the unions, and the public. Its work built on studies of
the status of state-employed women that actually predated
the formation of the Council in 1976 by five years.
Using the Hay point factor system, the task force study
"documented salary disparities between male-dominated and
female-dominated job classes and recommended that the
legislature appropriate money to eliminate the
disparities."[18] The cost--$26 million--was approximately
4 percent of the state's payroll.

Legislation followed in 1982, changing the personnel
law to establish a policy to provide equitable
compensation relationships between the classes of

employees and to establish a procedure for making comparability adjustments. In January 1983 the personnel department submitted its recommendations of job classes eligible for pay equity adjustments, and a biennial appropriation for $21.8 million was made. If a similar procedure is followed in 1985, total implementation will have been achieved within four years time. The actual distribution of salary increases is negotiated through collective bargaining. Eighty-six percent of Minnesota's state employees are covered under collective bargaining agreements.

The task force priority of getting the principle of pay equity established in the law was achieved. Senator Bergman chaired the Council on the Economic Status of Women, and recounts that they had "all of the players on the task force--the Department of Employee Relations, AFSCME, Chair of the Legislative Commission on Salaries and Pensions, members of the public, League of Women Voters--all groups concerned with the issue."[19] Second, they "set up a process where the Commissioner of Employee Relations would bring to our Commission on Employee Salaries those numbers of jobs where 70 percent of those classes are female. When pay equity is warranted, and the Commission will so establish, then an amount of money will be set aside in the budget to be targeted for pay equity."[20]

Spillover effects have occurred in Minnesota whereby the University of Minnesota has commenced conducting its own studies, and the council task force is meeting with representatives of local government. AFSCME, Bergman notes, wants action because of its legal responsibility to represent employees. AFSCME had "no choice but to bring these individual units of local government to court one by one." She adds that the council would rather see an "amicable process."[21]

Two important concepts in Bergman's statement warrant elaboration. First, even in jurisdictions that have a very narrowly defined scope of bargaining, comparable worth raises bargainable issues.[22] Thirty-one states have the duty of fair representation, including twenty-one of the twenty-five states that currently have studies. So unions in those states must be especially vigilant in representing their members or face being sued for nonrepresentation. The second important concept, inherent in her description, is the character of the Minnesota approach to problem solving; it is inclusive, rather than exclusive--inviting members of the public and interested parties to participate.[23] Further, state policymakers concerned with comparable worth took an interest in the potential for conflict at other jurisdictional levels and, typical of states Elazar terms Moralistic, saw the role of government as positive, participatory, and interventionist.

Minnesota, in effect, had a referendum on pay equity appropriation and processes in 1984 when the legislature extended pay equity to 855 cities, 87 counties, and 436 school districts. These jurisdictions have 163,000 workers, 56 percent of whom are female.[24]

Connecticut's approach to implementation has not been as open and discursive. Rather, it seems dominated by a staff-consultant-interest group monopoly over decision making. Legislators who are members of the advisory committee rarely attend meetings. Members of the public, or nonpartisan good government groups are not encouraged to attend the meetings. The private-sector members represent only personnel managers.

Technically, the survey component of the Connecticut study was to have been facilitated by a network of agency liaisons and union steward/delegates, but the surveys are the weakest link. After three years' work, it was noted in January 1984 that only 1,500 of the 2,550 job classifications had been surveyed; of these, 300 still had insufficient questionnaire return rates, and only 432 had been evaluated.[25]

In summary, Connecticut's implementation approach is heavily dominated by professional-interest group interaction, and lacks the involvement of legislative leaders and the interested public in keeping policy open and on track. Lagging questionnaire returns suggest that employees may have reservations about the intended use of the information. Handling the study as an administrative-union matter may facilitate technical processing but has raised credibility problems and some unspoken resistance.

Washington's administrative reaction to its three studies is hard to judge. Judge Tanner of the Federal District court in Washington found "the record is replete with contemporary letters, memorandums, and reports.../that indicate to this Court/ an administrative history that reflects knowledge by Defendant of sex discrimination in State employment since no later than March 24, 1982."[26] No conclusions can be drawn from this scant reference, and the matter most certainly will be the subject of appeals by the state. In the interim it appears that the sanction and an appropriation for comparable worth give notice from the legislature to the personnel department to implement the policies, at least to the extent that $1.5 million will allow.

SURVEY OF DIRECTORS OF STATE PERSONNEL

Davis and West's early work on comparable worth frames the research question that guided my survey of state personnel directors. If, as Sabatier and Mazmanian contend, "New programs require implementers who are not merely neutral but sufficiently persistent to develop new . . . procedures, and to enforce them in the face of resistance from target groups and from public officials,"[27] do state personnel directors have sufficient commitment to comparable worth to insure its political survival as a program? Davis and West surveyed 357 urban personnel managers to ascertain to what extent comparable worth as policy was favored; whether personal, organizational, institutional, or legal characteristics affected managers' opinions and specific policy preferences, including whether legislative, administrative, or judicial action was favored; and what barriers to implementation were perceived likely.

Davis and West found that there was moderate general support, 67 percent, for the premise that "traditional female jobs" were undervalued, and 52 percent of the respondents favored expanding "equal pay for equal jobs" to "equal pay for comparable jobs." The authors concluded that managers were more inclined to agree that there were economic inequities involved but were only cautiously supportive of comparable worth as a policy.

West and Davis then looked at a number of contextual factors, such as size of jurisdiction, population size, form of government, presence or absence of a state policy on comparable worth, and presence or absence of collective bargaining or affirmative action. Their findings were not consistent with their research expectations. "Individual perceptions of comparable worth /were/ largely unaffected by the presence or absence of a state policy or by the form of government." Most surprising was that there was a significant relationship between city size and support for comparable worth; contrary to what they had anticipated, directors in smaller communities were more favorably inclined.

For West and Davis, age and experience were related to receptiveness to the notion that women's jobs were undervalued--younger, less-experienced administrators tended toward being more favorable--but there was no significant relationship between these variables and acceptance of comparable worth. Women administrators were more supportive in general. As to hurdles, 60 percent of the respondents thought cost might be a major barrier, but the state of the art of job evaluation, or lack of support from union leaders or public officials were seen as less troublesome. The preference of 69 percent of the officials was to study their classification systems, 59 percent specifically desiring the use of factor-based job evaluation techniques; 73 percent were opposed to legislative remedies, and 83 percent to judicial remedies.[28]

The West and Davis survey is relevant because cities have had considerable comparable worth study activity. (See Appendix A.) The research also encourages speculation as to whether state personnel directors charged with administering comparable worth studies might differ from urban managers, or from state directors in states with no comparability policies. Even when one accepts Sabatier and Mazmanian's proposition that managerial commitment is crucial to implementation, there still exist limitations on knowing to what degree any given director of personnel or the chief wage and classification director really does influence initiation of policy or its implementation. There are simply a myriad of factors that can intervene. At a minimum these factors include the relative power and interest of the individual or group to whom the director is accountable (board, commission, governor, or some other chain of command); the degree of legislative sophistication, interest, and activism; the comprehensiveness of the state collective bargaining law and the tenor of labor relations in general; and finally, the director's experience, personal characteristics, and beliefs about his or her own administrative efficacy.

It is possible to control for some of these factors when analyzing responses to questions about policy choices and equity perceptions, and it is possible to extend the analysis to include environmental factors, such as population size, status of comparable worth activity, if any, and several political indicators. The political indicators could include the effect of political culture; policy innovativeness of the state; measures of formal gubernatorial power, for instance, whether the office can be held for more than one term; level of party competitiveness in the gubernatorial race; whether the legislature was well staffed and professionalized; the history of women's policy actions or proportion of women legislators; and whether there had been a civil service reform that affected structural organization. Analysis can include economic variables, such as the size of the state work force and payroll, state debt, and per capita income.

To explore these factors, the author sent questionnaires in the spring of 1984 to all fifty state personnel directors. The response rate was 82 percent. Of these forty-one responses from directors (or, in seven cases the chief administrative officer responsible for classification and pay), thirty-six proved ultimately usable as a data base. Respondents were predominantly male (75 percent), and their age distribution was: 30-40 years, 42 percent; 40-50, 19 percent; and over 50, 27 percent. Their years of experience in personnel administration ranged from under 10 years, 22 percent; through 10-20 years, 33 percent; 20-30 years, 30 percent; to over 40 years, 3 percent.[29]

Several questions were asked to measure the general level of agreement with the idea that women in government jobs were paid less than men in comparable jobs, and to ascertain whether the directors perceived women's jobs in the labor market generally to be undervalued as well.

Half the respondents indicated agreement with the idea that women in government are paid less than men for jobs that are comparable in knowledge and skills, mental demands, accountability, and working conditions; 22 percent disagreed; and 28 percent neither agreed nor disagreed. The perception of the degree of under- or overpayment of women in such jobs was queried. Half said women in government were paid somewhat to a lot less; 31 percent thought they were paid just about the same; and 11 percent thought they were paid somewhat or a lot more than men. Perceptions shifted slightly when asked if women's jobs were typically undervalued in the labor market. Here the percentage so believing rose to 58; disbelieving, 8 percent; and those with a foot in neither camp, 31 percent.[30]

Thirty-six percent of the states represented in the sample do not have a classification study using comparable worth factors; in another 36 percent a study is deemed likely; and 19 percent are either currently conducting or have completed studies. In 14 percent of the states studies had been considered and rejected by the legislature, but for 83 percent of the states, no study had been considered and subsequently rejected by the legislature.

Next came a question as to whether the director would recommend a study. Nineteen percent did not answer, 44 percent responded no, and 36 percent yes. The reasons given for not recommending were divided into major and minor. 25 percent thought litigation a major reason; 22 percent, lack of political consensus; 17 percent, absence of a specialized staff or resources to undertake the study; and 3 percent thought such studies detrimental rather than helpful to women.

A series of questions dealt with groups or individuals likely to be supporters or opponents of job evaluation studies using comparable worth factors. Eighty-one percent of the respondents thought unions or organizations representing public employees were likely to be supporters of comparable worth; 6 percent saw unions as neutral; and 3 percent believed that unions both support and oppose studies. Regarding women's political groups, 97 percent of the respondents saw such groups supporting comparable worth studies; 3 percent did not answer; and none perceived opposition emanating from women's political groups at all.[31]

Directors generally saw 53 percent of the governors supporting such studies, 33 percent being neutral on comparable worth, and only 6 percent opposed. A slightly more negative image was held relative to legislators: 53 percent, supportive; 25 percent, neutral; and 14 percent opposed--but none strongly. Next in level of support, in the directors' opinions, came personnel administrators, who tied with federal agencies and officials at 39 percent supportive, and 36 percent neutral. Personnel administrators were seen to oppose studies using comparable worth by 19 percent of the respondents; federal agencies and officials, by 11 percent.

When asked to rate their preferences, from most preferred to least, 67 percent would encourage women in the state employ to move into nontraditional occupations; only 3 percent saw this as a least-preferred alternative. The next option, doing nothing and waiting for change to occur, was the preference of 42 percent and the least preferred by 36 percent. Commencing joint labor-management studies of classifications with more than 70 percent incumbency by one sex was the most preferred by 36 percent and least preferred by 44 percent. The last choice, retraining or employing classification and compensation specialists experienced in ferreting out sex bias in evaluation procedures, was the most preferred for 56 percent of the respondents, and the least preferred by 22 percent.

The next series of questions had respondents rank the likelihood of happening for the items of which they had just expressed a preference. Forty-seven percent believed that "encouraging women to move into nontraditional jobs" was quite likely; 17 percent, least likely. Only 23 percent thought that "doing nothing" would be most likely; 33 percent rated it unlikely. Thirty-eight percent rated the "commencing joint labor-management" studies most likely; the same percentage predicted it to be least likely. "Retraining or employing specialists" to detect sex bias in evaluation procedures also came out in a tie: 36 percent for most likely to happen, and 36 percent for least likely.

To probe what political and economic factors of the states may have influenced the directors' responses to the questionnaire, the states were categorized by study adoption status: non-study adopters, study adopters with comparable worth legislation, and study adopters without comparable worth legislation. Correlations between study-status of a state and the political and economic factors enumerated in Chapter 4 were ascertained for each state. The general correlation of study states with legislative professionalism was .50, with governor's power .48, and with unionization .47. Additionally, years of experience of the respondents correlated with study status at .40. States whose directors had not responded to the questionnaire, with the exception of one, ranked in the lowest quartile for legislative professionalism.

Where Davis and West found 52 percent of their urban personnel manager respondents amenable to comparable worth measures and 67 percent agreeing that traditional women's jobs were undervalued, the state director study here reported found only 50 percent agreeing that women in government were paid less for comparable knowledge and skills, mental demands, accountability, and working conditions. A slightly higher percentage (58) viewed the labor market as undervaluing women's work.

When comparing the directors' support for comparable worth by age and experience, there appears to be more among those with up to twenty years' experience. Age and sex seem not to make a difference.

CONCLUSIONS

What can be concluded from these research findings? First, the directors are more supportive than not of the idea that women in government are not paid comparable to the jobs they do, and the labor market is generally less generous. It is probably fair to say that by Sabatier and Mazmanian's standards this does not constitute a strong showing of potential commitment to predict program success in implementation.

Still, the directors' perceptions of who influences compensation policy in their states had a few surprises: the governor and the legislature were rated influential by 86 percent and 89 percent of the respondents, respectively, which was expected. What was not expected was the perceived support of the governor for comparable worth studies (53 percent, versus 33 percent neutral), the high support of the legislature (53 percent supportive versus 25 percent neutral), and that 52 percent thought the unions to be most influential in pay policies.

Interesting, too, and a little surprising is how only one of the directors' preferences ranked most desired, "having women move into nontraditional jobs," also was most predicted to be a likely event. The least preferred, "commencing joint labor-management studies," moved into the second-most-likely category; and the option supported by 42 percent of the respondents as most desirable, "doing nothing," became the least likeliest.

Thirty-six percent of the respondents thought recommending a study unwise because there existed no political consensus on the issue as yet in their state. This compares with the 19 percent of Davis and West's urban personnel managers who cited lack of political consensus. Indeed, the high percentages of perceived support of the issue among unions, women's political groups, the governors, legislators, and personnel administrators suggest a good deal more backing for the issue than might have been inferred absent this study.

It is difficult to know exactly what level of commitment is necessary and sufficient to carry through a program of this type. From this survey, however, there is every indication that the directors are sufficiently informed about the level of support for the issue among elected policymakers and unions to carry studies forward if prescribed by executive order, statute, or collective bargaining. It is more than likely that the directors do not perceive comparable worth in any normative sense, but that their implementation activities would spring from more pragmatic considerations; that is, that comparable worth is perceived to be more supported than opposed by those political figures who make compensation policy in their states--the governor, the legislature, and the unions. Further, there is every reason to believe that where the formal powers of the governor are extensive, and legislative professionalism is high, study adoption and implementation will proceed apace.

NOTES

1. E.C. Hargrove, The Missing Link: The Study of Implementation of Social Policy (Washington, DC: July 1975), p. 107. Emphasis is mine.
2. J.L. Pressman and A. Wildavsky, Implementation (Berkeley, CA, 1973), p. 180.
3. Table No. 795, "Number of Governors by Party, 1960-1982," U.S. Bureau of the Census, Statistical Abstract (1983), p. 496.
4. D. Dresang, "Diffusion of Civil Service Reform," Review of Public Personnel Administration 22 (Spring 1982), pp. 41-42.
5. C. Levine, "Hidden Hazards of Retrenchment," The Bureaucrat 10 (Fall 1981), pp.4-5.
6. C. Levine and F. Nigro, "The Public Personnel System: Can Juridical Administration and Manpower Management Coexist?" Public Administration Review 35 (January/February 1975), pp. 98-107.
7. D.R. Cooke, "Developments in State Personnel," Book of the States (Lexington, KY, 1982), pp. 309-44.
8. J. Nalbandian and D. Klinger, "The Politics of Public Personnel Administration: Towards Theoretical Understanding," Public Administration Review 41 (September/October 1981), p. 541.
9. D. Steward, "Managing Competing Claims: An Ethical Framework for Human Relations Decision-Making," Public Administration Review 44 (January/February, 1984), pp. 14-22.
10. J.M. Shafritz, A.C. Hyde, and D.H. Rosenbloom, Personnel Management in Government, 2d ed. (New York, 1981), p. 56.
11. S. Welch and K. Thompson, "The Impact of Federal Incentives on State Policy Innovation," American Journal of Political Science 24 (November 1980), p. 722.
12. The discussion of organizational levels that follows is from Nalbandian and Klinger, "The Politics of Public Personnel Administration," pp. 541-49.
13. Shafritz, Hyde, and Rosenbloom, Personnel Management in Government, p. 23.
14. Sharkansky summarizes Elazar's description of the relationship between culture, and participation, bureaucracy, and government programs in a "linear continua: from Moralism to Individualism to Traditionalism," and combinations of emphasis falling in between. I. Sharkansky, "Utility of Elazar's Political Culture," Polity 2 (Fall 1969), p. 70.
15. Taped remarks of Representative Jennifer Belcher, State of Washington, at the Carnegie Foundation National Conference of Women State Legislators, 2-3 December 1983, San Diego, CA.
16. Taped remarks of Senator Eleanor Lee, State of

Minnesota, at the Carnegie Foundation National Conference of Women State Legislators, 2-3 December 1983, San Diego, CA.

17. Taped remarks of Senator Linda Bergman, State of Minnesota, at the Carnegie Foundation National Conference of Women State Legislators, 2-3 December 1983, San Diego, CA.

18. "Pay Equity--The Minnesota Experience," Commission on the Economic Status of Women background paper (St. Paul, May 1984), p. 1.

19. Remarks of Bergman. See note 18.

20. Ibid.

21. Ibid.

22. W. Kay and M. Carol Stevens, "Potential Impact of Concept of Comparable Worth on Public Sector Bargaining," National Public Employment Reporter 14 (March 1982), pp. 25-36. The duty of fair representation means a union must represent all members of a bargaining unit, impartially and without invidious discrimination. An employee may seek remedy from a union for perfunctory, arbitrary, or discriminatory treatment or for acting in bad faith.

23. This openness in personnel management where collective bargaining issues are involved is atypical, and is an area that deserves concerted research and discussion. Couturier and Schick note in their article on civil service reform in the 1980s that "it is ironic that collective bargaining is about the only major policy decision making process where public access to information is espoused openly by many practitioners as detrimental rather than beneficial to public policy." They conclude: "Such secrecy makes it all the more difficult to hold public officials accountable for labor relations policies. By contrast, no one would think of adopting the annual budget without benefit of public hearings and discussion." J.J. Couturier and R.P. Schick, "The Second Century of Civil Service Reform: An Agenda for the 1980s," in Public Personnel Administration: Problems and Prospects, ed. S.W. Hays and R.C. Kearney (Englewood Cliffs, NJ, 1983), p. 325. See also R.P. Schick and J.J. Couturier, The Public Interest in Government Labor Relations (Cambridge, MA, 1977).

24. Testimony of N. Rothchild, Commissioner of Employee Relations, State of Minnesota, "Overview of Pay Equity Initiative, 1974-1984." Prepared for the U.S. Commission on Civil Rights Consultation on Comparable Worth, Washington, DC, 7 June 1984, p. 19.

25. State of Connecticut Job Evaluation Program Annual Status Report, submitted by Job Evaluation Unit, Personnel Division, Department of Administrative Services (Hartford, January 1974).

26. American Federation of State, County, and Municipal Employees vs. State of Washington, Docket No.

C 82-465T DLR (Washington, DC, 15 December 1983) D6.

27. See analysis of P. Sabatier and D. Mazmanian, "The Implementation of Public Policy: A Framework of Analysis," Policy Studies Journal 8 Special Issue, 1980, pp. 538-60 in C.D. Davis and J. West, "Jobs, Dollars and Gender: An Analysis of the Comparable Worth Issue in Urban Areas," paper presented at Annual Meeting, American Society for Public Administration, New York, April 1983.

28. Ibid., pp. 4-11.

29. This group of personnel administrators is much more concentrated in higher age and experience ranges than the Davis and West sample of 347 urban managers in "Jobs, Dollars, and Gender," paper presented at Annual Meeting, American Society for Public Administration, New York, 1983, Table 3.

30. This finding of 58 percent of the respondents agreeing that the labor market typically undervalued women's jobs is particularly notable in conjunction with findings of West of a sample of 403 urban personnel managers conducted in 1979. The question in this research concerned the relationship between support for unionization with agreement for a policy that public wage policies should be adjusted to the salaries and benefits offered in the private sector in preference to their being negotiated through collective bargaining. Sixty-two percent of those who were low in their general support of unions preferred adopting private-sector levels; 48 percent of those only moderately supportive of unions disagreed; and 69 percent of those supportive of unions disagreed. See J. West, "Public Sector Collective Bargaining and Merit: Accommodation or/ Conflict?" paper presented at American Society for Public Administration, Hartford, CT, 1981, p. 7 and Table 2. In all, 46 percent of the sample disagreed with a "policy designed to adjust employees' compensation to private-sector levels automatically."

31. This finding of no perceived opposition to comparable worth by women's political groups is particularly interesting, considering that only 64 percent of the states responding had been ERA ratifiers. It is possible that the nontransferability effect of women's policy issues noted by Gelb and Palley is operative here, and that even in those states where women's political groups opposed to the ERA more than likely contributed to high levels of political conflict, there is no spillover or aggregative effect to this issue--at least not at this time.

6
The Future of Comparable Worth

If, as Schattschneider believes, it is the weak who ordinarily desire to socialize conflict, the crucial problem in politics becomes the management of conflict once an issue becomes salient. How the issue is defined, who is involved, the resources available, and the displacement of conflict are all shifting instruments of political strategy. Controlling the definition of an issue is paramount and depends on how specific or abstract it is in goals and symbolic references, and its present and future impact on society. Technical complexity and whether an issue sets precedents also act as contingencies that speed or retard its development and diffusion. Social movement organizations differ from interest groups in the way they can mobilize resources to define issues that have a societal impact.[1]

The story of comparable worth related thus far chronicles the development of two social movements: the pay equity movement and civil service reform. Both movements embody sets of ideas about societal needs, and have fostered actions and policy interventions that contain an identifiable ideological nucleus. This chapter relates how the two movements converge, with what consequences, and how comparable worth's definition will shape the interaction of the two and affect the realization of their separate goals. The chapter first offers some background of national presidential election-year events that ghost the issue, proceeds to a general description of how the issue can be framed, offers suggestions for why one definition should take precedence over another, and then analyzes the cost and opportunities involved. The chapter concludes with speculation on whether the conflict over comparable worth will increase appreciation for the social value of work and representative government or, conversely, plunge unwary participants into experimentation with ill-defined goals and no hope of responsible administration.

There is a good deal of journalistic speculation over whether the Reagan administration has plans to sabotage comparable worth by using post-election Justice Department intervention against AFSCME in the pending State of Washington suit.[2] Some Reagan administration officials have suggested that the administration engage in covert activities "pitting union against union and both against radical feminist groups."[3] More than likely, the pre-election sensitivity of this administration to the electoral volatility of women voters--the "gender gap"--will warrant caution.[4] The administration will probably just continue to enlarge more low-key strategies of incapacitating current federal boards and agencies through the appointment process. This has proved most efficient in quieting those boards and agencies noted for their objectivity and vigilance in matters of civil rights and discrimination. Current boards that bear the Reagan imprimatur of conservatism include the U.S. Commission on Civil Rights, the National Labor Relations Board, the Equal Employment Opportunity Commission, the Justice Department, and if a second term ensues, the U.S. Supreme Court.[5] Reagan's administrative strategies raise questions of the separation of administration, ideology, and politics in a free society.

Elsewhere in the administration, the rationale for opposing comparable worth, offered by a Department of Justice spokesman in January 1984, included a professed skepticism over job evaluation techniques; a belief that low pay for women meant not necessarily employer discrimination but a possible lack of motivation on the part of those women who neither sought nor took advantage of opportunities; and an acknowledgement that the administration had no clear idea of what constituted a remedy. As the election drew closer and women's groups remonstrated to Reagan regarding his insensitivity toward working women, statements to the press about possible strategies against comparable worth stopped. On the other side of the fence, speculation about how to convert disenchantment of women into voting blocs increased among Democratic party presidential candidates, who, additionally, endorsed comparable worth.

Important as presidential appointments and Justice Department intervention are to any policy issue, there are myriad other issues to consider that should be incorporated into its definition or excised.

HOW COMPARABLE WORTH IS DEFINED AND
WHO IS INVOLVED

What is necessary at this juncture in the development of comparable worth is a sustained analysis of shifting judicial climates and the resulting growth of constituencies comprising organized private interests, particularly unions, elected officials, and government agencies. Policy analysis, therefore, was used in this study to offer benchmarks by which to judge the importance of social change. While policy analysis is limited in that it centers on whether an issue is resolved in its immediate context,[6] it can nevertheless highlight the normative dimensions of an administrative issue and offer guidance on framing it so as to yield reasonable predictions of its impact.

There are many opinions on what comparable worth represents as policy. Some would have us believe that the issue, at root, is one of domestic roles versus working roles for women; that it is not a political issue of role equity but a personal issue of role change.[8] Some who reason in this way envisage the agenda of pay equity advocates to be "the feminization of the labor market," making the workplace more like women--caring, people oriented, perceptive--and that this bespeaks hostility to both capitalism and the male ethos because workplaces "simply demand...'masculine' behavior from employees."[9] Others try to link its definition to the advent of EEO/Affirmative Action or to depict it as a triumph of meritocracy or credentialism. Still others speak of its technology as human engineering or socialism--all extremely volatile issues in their own right.[10]

The constellation of opinions does not help to frame the issue within a policy spectrum. What is more useful is observation. Why comparable worth arose, who sponsored and followed through on it, where it was diffused and what changes it was directed toward all clearly point to its dominance as a legislative issue rather than a judicial or administrative one.

"At its heart," Nina Rothchild, commissioner of employee relations for the State of Minnesota, responded in questioning, "comparable worth represents the increasing rate of political participation of women."[11] Many of the issue's sponsors are seasoned women legislators and personnel of state commissions on the status of women who have a decade of experience in elective state politics.[12]

To frame, or define the issue, then: Comparable worth is the outward and visible form of the growth in numbers and strength of women in state legislatures, and the organization of women in the state employ in their own economic and political interest. There is no socialist conspiracy, there are no radical programs of human engineering or for redistributing wealth, there is just representative politics by women on a women's policy issue in a year of gender politics. Within those parameters of definition, all suggestions of linkages to sex role or credentialism, meritocracy or socialism, are essentially discounting the momentum of the pay equity movement's ability to tap symbolic resources of the feminization of poverty at the same time that it meets state government's needs to upgrade and professionalize the management of its personnel systems. It is these two factors--the objective status of women in society, and the desire to modernize and invigorate state government human resource management--that have brought the issue beyond interest-group politics into the realm of ideology and mass movement.

There are two other policy choices: comparable worth could be defined as a judicial or administrative issue rather than a legislative one. Why not do so? Will AFSCME v. State of Washington dominate the characterization of the issue? It is arguable that by the time a final judicial determination is made, it will not materially affect the job evaluation study findings or implementation plans conducted by the states or localities in the interim.

One notion, which may spring from the experience of the women's rights movement of the early 1960s, is that if women wait for the Supreme Court to rule, they will have lost not only the initiative in political events, but the ability to act as well. Martha Griffiths, speaking as an attorney who once thought the "way to handle equal rights cases was to bring case after case under the Constitution before the courts," /came/ to the conclusion, "after many years of reading cases, that the Supreme Court was untouchable and unteachable." She then turned her considerable energies to other legislative strategies.[13]

Pragmatically, judicial relief, if granted, will be limited to those cases on appeal, the most egregious situations. The prognosis for retroactive relief or for the Supreme Court's pressing states and municipalities beyond their capacity to pay, or entering into any determination of standards of evaluation for jobs is slim indeed. However, with a strong state statute or local ordinance, and a good study, relief is prospective.

AFSCME v. Washington appeals will consume five years, and
more than likely may be less shattering in terms of
precedents for the states by the time of decision than is
envisaged in 1984.

Any number of proponents have tried to define
comparable worth as an exclusively moral issue, witness
the term "pay equity." While subnational governments
seem ill equipped to weigh questions about responsibility
for the apparent lag in women's compensation, appropriate
remedies, and who will pay, they are in the process of
doing so. By prescribing equal protection under the law,
collective bargaining, and merit and evaluation systems
for employees, they set the standards by which they
themselves will be judged.

Politics and political administration are different
from private pursuits and generic administration.
Government policies should represent some consideration
of ethical and moral suasion in content and process. It
is on this higher plane that the question of comparable
worth may well be resolved.[14] However, all concerned
should assess which "face" of comparable worth they are
dealing with--the ideological or methodological--and be
prepared to respond accordingly. The arguments that try
to dress what is essentially an economic matter in
"moral-issue" clothing to achieve ideological supremacy
will almost certainly incur more problems than solutions.
Social policies, directed by moral concern for those on
the margin of social, political, and economic life--be
they women, blacks, Hispanics, migrant workers,
unemployed and unskilled youth, or industrial workers
experiencing job displacement and deskilling--are
appropriate.

However, establishing that women do less well than
men economically, especially when jobs are segregated,
does not constitute conclusive evidence of discrimination. Other factors related to sex role--discontinuities
in employment related to homemaking, pay differentials
because of unionization, multiplicity of unions, specialized skill markets, supply factors--affect the economic
viability of women workers as well.[15]

Would not a legal determination cast these questions
of the morality of comparable worth as a remedy for wage
differentials and sex-segregated jobs in bold relief--
-giving a definitive answer once and for all? Some would
argue that "there is a negative, not a positive correlation between laws and moral behavior; that as the former
proliferate, the latter decline." This view suggests
that the law in reality "is a body of negative sanctions
that prescribes and proscribes social behavior. The law

can never reward directly. It can reward only indirectly by punishing offenders and thus 'protecting' the general public." Foster argues persuasively that "moral decisions are value-based...content and context-specific, legal decisions are just the opposite: procedure-based decisions that are dependent upon historical precedent."[16]

Those proponents who would define comparable worth exclusively as a moral issue may see it as the ideological forerunner of a mass movement of working women that will sweep aside vestiges of job segregation and wage differentials, and portend new approaches to how the value of work will be defined and wealth redistributed. Ideological approaches are shortcuts to communicating with diverse populations who have neither the time nor the interest to be personally involved in political events. But ideological approaches can operate against advocates as well.[17] The possibility of sweeping change is probably unlikely in a fragmented political system with 8,000 jurisdictional units making rules governing the terms and conditions of employment.

Popularizing the topic to communicate its importance runs the risk of distortion through simplification to appeal to what Edelman thinks is characteristic of large numbers of people in our society: thinking "in terms of stereotypes, /unable to/ recognize or tolerate /ambiguity; responding/ chiefly to symbols that over-simplify and distort."[18] Within a framework of mass movements and community conflict, resolution of complex issues can turn on the ability to distort, ridicule and "create a reasonable doubt in the public mind."[19]

Proponents in the State of Washington were not helped by the issue's popularization in the press. Peirce reports that Geoffrey Cowley, a writer for the Seattle Weekly, could make fun of the subjective grounds on which the state's study was based, calling it the work of a "team of metaphysicians." Peirce continues, "Cowley added in a Washington Monthly article: 'Major civil-rights battles would turn on such questions as whether error-free typing is a greater corporate asset than leak-free plumbing, or whether sitting at a VDT places a greater strain on Betty's eyes than pipefitting places on Jack's back.'"[20]

Indeed, early and persistent ideologically based criticism of comparable worth has emanated from anti feminist Phyllis Schlafly, much along the lines reported in the OPM memorandum cited earlier of pitting worker against worker. Schlafly tries to characterize comparable worth as "demanding that women working 9-5

clerical jobs in safe, clean offices, heated in winter
and air-conditioned in summer, should receive equal wages
with police and fire fighters who work in dangerous jobs,
unpleasant conditions...who risk their lives day after
day to keep our cities safe."[21]

Feminist political advisers should not discount
Schlafly. She represents what Brady and Tedin call "a
rare phenomenon--an organized women's movement which has
experienced reasonable political success."[22] If
comparable worth becomes embroiled in ideological frames
of reference, the mass media may once again "give
legitimacy to the opposition by covering their media
events and spokesmen equally," as Daniels and Darcy found
with their study of the ERA ratification process.[23]
Boles's research suggests that so long as rebuttal is
swift and public by legislative and political figures,[24]
the conflict stays within bounds and can accommodate
solution. But the pressure toward .hyperbole will
probably continue among those who hold conflicting views
on the issue.[25]

It is possible that comparable worth is part of the
congeries of women's policy issues that have incurred
setbacks in recent Supreme Court decisions, such as those
concerning affirmative action plans and Title IX.[26] But
one or two decisions do not necessarily unravel the
"legislative framework" constructed over the past 17
years to produce equal economic opportunity.[27] The courts
move slowly; their remedies are uncertain. It behooves
one to consider what benefits might materialize in
immediate and tangible ways from defining comparable
worth as a legislative issue rather than seeking judicial
or bargaining remedies.[28] When one lays aside the
potential for community conflict that may not find
support because of comparable worth's adherence to
management norms, one finds that the overriding benefit
of such a definition is to create continuous public
oversight and participation through study and programs
created by elected officials who must answer for their
wage policies to the public.

To make comparable worth a solely administrative
issue would be to accelerate the trend noted by Frederick
Mosher toward "more reliance on negotiation, persuasion,
rewards," which, of course, would be particularly
expected and appropriate to collective bargaining. But
he cautions that "extension and intensification of
influence of pressure from interest groups on...policy
administration /especially single interest groups,
increases the/ possibility of political pressures...at
the lower levels of administration...appealed through
interest groups...to the highest level."[29] With only

126

vague guidelines, and a highly volatile and potentially
expensive issue, there may be a tendency to try to shift
the issue to a solely administrative arena, and apply
what Lambright, in another context, calls a
"technological fix." Lambright describes that the
"stakes of actors may be economic, bureaucratic, or
ideological...a given agency is a sponsor, manager, host
and defender of a certain technology. Unless careful, a
captive of its own programs."[30]

Many of personnel policy outcomes are implemented
through bargaining, but as policy analysts have found in
studying implementation of federal policies in the
states, authorizations and incentives do not insure
compliance or control; they achieve only the opportunity
to bargain.[31]

There are more immediate and tangible benefits, at
the moment, to be derived from defining comparable worth
as a legislative issue rather than seeking judicial or
bargaining remedies. First, as the survey reported in
Chapter 5 attests, there are positive signals from those
individuals and groups responsible for fiscal management
and compensation policies in the states--the governor,
the legislature, and the unions--so that pilot studies
are possible. Second, remedy can come in many forms.
For example, two procedural changes seem to be gaining
currency in theoretical works and personnel practice.
The first is that because unions have won National Labor
Relations Board sanction for bargaining over the
procedural aspects of performance appraisal systems,[32]
and because job evaluation and wage determination
mechanisms are "neither value-free nor scientifically
derived," affected groups should strive for greater
participation in job evaluation--through collectively
bargained contracts or part of traditional merit
systems--and remove the "influence of experts."[33]

The second procedural change is job redesign, which
offers a comprehensive approach to ending discrimination.
In theory, organizations can redesign job classes;
enlarge the complexity, scope, and responsibility of
jobs; construct career ladders; and provide on-the-job
training to facilitate upward integration rather than
merely make salary changes.[34] In practice, however,
upward mobility plans using job redesign have encountered
union hostility in the public sector over the potential
cooptation of individuals, and suspicioned limiting of
collectively bargained benefits. Again, when we look at
what the survey of state personnel directors tells us,
the policy prediction they thought most likely to
materialize was "encouraging women in government to move
into nontraditional jobs." This does not necessarily

mean standpattism; there was a category for "doing nothing." It is more likely to mean that job redesign as a matter of policy will become more popular.

It can be predicted, based on the experience of some states, that in large centralized personnel systems, objective job evaluation operations would probably be isolated as separate technical units, much like EEO-Affirmative Action, collective bargaining, and other controversial activities.[35] Such units would have as much access and credibility in higher policy circles as the systems directors believe is politically expedient or administratively necessary. The isolation would be a safeguard against the politically vulnerable appointed directors' being held directly responsible for the units' work. Distance would allow some selection and discretion in approval or disapproval of unit products. Union or employee members of advisory committees and select evaluation teams deployed by such studies handle the shirtsleeve work of scrutinizing classifications job by job to reach some consensus over benchmark positions. Where patterns break down is at the implementation stage when dollar figures are attached to the classification systems newly "certified" as scientifically derived and equitable. Here new strategies and arenas of activity become relevant.[36]

CONCLUSIONS

Examining and upgrading classifications of work that have social value that can be established and justified to management and labor is long overdue. The greatest casualties of a solely ideological approach to the issue will be the women caught in the narrow band of occupations that are becoming more automated. If comparable worth retards the integration of women into nontraditional employment, it will be a conservative doctrine indeed.[37] The author concurs with Ray Marshall that job evaluation "is not precise--it is inherently judgmental, but it is an established technique and comparable worth cases would involve no more judgment than ordinarily is involved in wage and salary administration."[38] Much of the determination of the approach to change--conflict or measured cooperation consistent with the public interest--will be by managers who design and implement appropriate remedies. It is hoped that the legislative oversight will be sufficient to encourage that such evaluations be undertaken by extremely competent staff who are unequivocally supported from the top, and who have a scale of operations large enough to make meaningful occupational comparisons but small enough to take individual fears into consideration. Regardless of size, such operations require employee participation that is flexibly designed, well informed, and that operates in good faith.[39]

NOTES

1.   See E. E. Schattschneider, _The Semisovereign People_ (Hinsdale, IL, 1960), pp. 36,40,69,170, and R.W. Cobb and C.D. Elder, _Participation in American Politics_ (Boston, 1972), pp. 96-102.

2.   Pear outlines a plan for a friend of the court intervention petition on the boards at the Justice Department awaiting White House approval. Attributions to the counsel of the Office of Management and Budget of planning strategies to undermine comparable worth through shaping civil rights policy add further speculation to what awaits the November 1984 election. See R. Pear, "Administration May Challenge Pay Rule," _New York Times_, 22 January 1984, pp. 1, 16. Sabotage is consistent with what Newland terms an "ideological political administration." In personnel policies the relationship of responsible political control has shifted to responsiveness to an "ideological political administration," with effects of retrenchment, a diminution of equal opportunity/affirmative action, and lack of institutional support for the senior executive service. Newland outlines Reagan's general agenda in the example of his conversion of EO/AA to eo/aa. First are the president's personal views regarding eo/aa: it is an individual matter. Next came agency funding cuts that reduced expertise and activities, followed by a demotion from the office of the Director of Personnel Management (OPM) to two levels below. Newland fears the concentration of both policy and implementation "in the hands of politicians," and believes that constitutional government's practice of having politically elected and appointed officials and career personnel working together in different roles of policy formulation and implementation has been observed more when it serves political goals. See C.A. Newland, "A Mid-Term Appraisal--the Reagan Administration," _Public Administration Review_ 43 (January/February 1983), p. 19. The new director of the EEOC has generally been unresponsive to processing comparable worth cases and has testified to House committees several times in the past two years that his agency is studying the issue.

3.   The strategy of creating union conflict over comparable worth reportedly arose from a policy memorandum to U.S. Office of Personnel Management

Director Donald J. Define from his deputy associate
director, James L. Byrnes, suggesting ways to counteract
the effect of the imminent passage of H.R. 4599, "Federal
Employees' Pay Equity Act of 1984," sponsored by Rep.
Mary Rose Oakar. See C. Peterson and M. Causey, "Can the
GOP 'Create Disorder'?" Washington Post National Weekly,
11 June 1984, p. 11.

4. For an excellent journalistic summary of the
political impact of the "gender gap" on the Reagan
administration, see D. Kirschten, "The Reagan Reelection
Campaign Hopes 1984 Will Be the Year of the Women,"
National Journal 16 (June 1984), pp. 1082-85; and J.
Perlez, "Women, Power and Politics," New York Times
Magazine, 24 June 1984, pp. 23-26,28,30-31,72,76. For a
technical summary of the Washington Post-ABC News Polls
concerning gender and opinions toward party and national
candidates, see B. Sussman, "Most Explanations of the
Gender Gap Don't Hold Up," Washington Post National
Weekly, 20 February 1984, p. 36.

5. For a view of two commissioners who currently
form the minority opinion on the U.S. Commission on Civil
Rights since its November 30, 1983 reorganization, see B.
C. Ramirez and M. F. Berry, "Civil Rights Commission
Majority vs. a National Consensus," New York Times, 26
February 1984. For discussion of the import of Reagan
appointments to the EEOC, see E. Holsendolph, "Skills,
Not Bias, Seen as Key for Jobs," New York Times, 3 July
1984, p. 5, and F. Barringer, "A Bureaucratic Brawl
Splits the EEOC," Washington Post National Weekly, 26
March 1984, pp. 30-31.

6. K. Kramer, "Seeds of Success and Failure: Policy
Development and Implementation of the 1978 Civil Service
Reform Act," Review of Public Personnel Administration 2
(Spring 1982), pp. 5-20.

7. E. Johansen, "Managing the Revolution," Review
of Public Personnel Administration 4 (Spring, 1984), p.
17.

8. B. Berger, "Occupational Segregation and the
Earnings Gap: Comparable Worth at Odds with American
Realities," paper delivered at the U.S. Commission on
Civil Rights Consultation on Comparable Worth, 7 June
1984.

9. R. Flick, "New Feminism and the World of Work,"
Public Interest, Spring 1983, p. 43.

10. See debate over meritocracy and affirmative
action in D. Bell, "On Meritocracy and Equality," Public
Interest 29 (Fall), pp. 29-68; M.M. Lepper, "Affirmative
Action: A Tool for Effective Personnel Management," in
Public Personnel Administration, ed. S. Hays and R.
Kearney, (Englewood Cliffs, NJ, 1983); pp. 217-45; and
M.M.Lepper, "The Status of Women in the U.S., 1976: Still
Looking for Justice and Equity," Public Administration
Review 36 (September/October 1976), pp. 365-69. Also see

130

views on the relationship of credentialism to comparable
worth in Berger, "Occupational Segregation and the
Earnings Gap."
    11.   Testimony of N.   Rothchild at the U.S.
Commission on Civil Rights Consultation on Comparable
Worth, 7 June 1984.
    12.   K. Burstein, "Notes from a Political Career,"
in B. Cummings and V. Schuch, eds., Women Organizing: An
Anthology (Metuchen, NJ, 1979), pp. 49-60, relates the
"benefits for the general polity from the fact that women
are not warmly accepted into the /legislative/ club, that
they are not easily assimilated as 'one of the boys.'" If
the rule of legislative career ascension is protecting
one another from outside criticism, the penalty for
observing it is that often it "takes so long to reach
leadership positions that one forgets, on attaining
power, the original reasons that sent one into politics."
She concludes, "Women, excluded from the climb from the
beginning, outsiders by biological accident, have no
stake in preserving the game intact. More, they are
likely to regard it with a sufficiently jaundiced eye to
make loud noises about its obvious failings." She calls
this "the naked emperor phenomenon" (pp. 51-52).
Burstein, now commissioner of civil service for the State
of New York, was writing of her experiences in 1972 as a
state legislator seven years earlier. Her perspective, I
submit, is most common among seasoned women legislators.
She wrote that by "raising issues, widening the grounds
of discussion, protesting the closed, insular nature of
legislative activity../she and her women colleagues made
/major contributions" (p. 53).
    13.   F.S.   Ingersoll, "Former Congresswomen Look
Back," in Women in Washington, I. Tinker ed. (Beverly
Hills, CA:1983), p. 199.
    14.   E.Johansen, "Managing the Revolution," p. 17.
    15.   E.   Johansen, "Comparable Worth: Surveying the
Controversy," The Bureaucrat 13 (Spring 1984), p. 13.
16. G.D. Foster, "Law, Morality and the Public Servant,"
Public Administration Review 41 (January/February 1981),
pp. 29-31.
    17.   For a lucid commentary on the effect of
ideology and community conflict, see J.K. Boles, The
Politics of the Equal Rights Amendment, (New York, 1979),
regarding the defeat of the Equal Rights Amendment. The
issue was broadened to appeal to more subgroups and
introduced the abstract terms "equality" and "justice."
It was "perceived as being of general and enduring social
significance." So long as it was an interest-group
issue, ratification proceeded at a pace with other
constitutional amendments, according to M. Daniels and R.
Darcy, "As Time Goes By: The Arrested Diffusion of the
Equal Rights Amendment," unpublished paper, 1984. When
the scope of the conflict broadened to include ad hoc

women's groups who had limited experience with interest-group politics and were not bounded by its conventions and rules, the "dynamics of community conflict became controlling," according to Boles (p.10). Without controversy, and with group pressure in one direction, she hypothesizes, lawmakers generally vote with the group. But when controversy is injected, they are more likely to postpone action, and weigh the relative merits of both sides. If the issue is argued on technical or legal grounds in addition, with contradictory experts, decision making by lawmakers can slow appreciably. If ideology and sentiment infuse the debate, and established community leaders withdraw or "become neutralized," legislators may postpone action indefinitely.

18. M. Edelman, Symbolic Uses of Politics (Urbana, Ill. 1964), p. 31.

19. J.K. Boles, Politics of the Equal Rights Amendment, p. 18.

20. N.R. Peirce, "Comparable Pay--Comparable Dedication?" Hartford Courant, 29 April 1984, p. C4.

21. P. Schlafly, "Equal Pay for Comparable Worth," Woman Constitutionalist 24 (September 1983), p. 2.

22. D.W. Brady and K. Tedin, "Ladies in Pink: Religion and Political Ideology in the Anti-ERA Movement," Social Science Quarterly 56 (March 1976), p. 564.

23. M. Daniels and R. Darcy, "As Time Goes By," p. 3.

24. "Lawmaker and Mrs. Schlafly Clash over Equal Pay Issue," New York Times, 5 April 1984, reports on a congressional hearing at which Schlafly attempted to tie comparable worth to women's "envy of wages paid to truckdrivers, janitors and firefighters." She drew a quick retort from Representative Mary Rose Oakar, who reportedly said, "Phyllis, please don't try to confuse the issue. The issue is not taking a nickel away from a firefighter or an electrician. We don't want to lessen any man's salary in any way, shape or form."

25. For a particularly bewildering example of linkage of several topics to the issue see S. Garment, "Comparable Worth: Stepping to Same Old Drummer," Wall Street Journal, 6 June 1984.

26. D. Gilliam, "Oyez. Oyez." Washington Post, 14 June 1982, p. 1; "The Court Strains to Make Work: Why Did It Have to Decide the Seniority Case at All?" New York Times (editorial), 14 June 1984; F. Barbash and K. Sawyer, "A New Era of 'Race Neutrality' in Hiring? Justice Department says Memphis Ruling Reopens Many Affirmative Action Plans," Washington Post National Weekly, 25 June 1984, p. 32; and B. Packwood discusses the import of the Supreme Court decision on Title IX if the Congress does not come forth with additional remedies

as "the dismantling /of/ more than 20 years of civil
rights progress." New York Times, 20 April 1984, p. A
27.

27. Sara G. Burr, "Women and Work" in The Women's
Annual, ed. B. Haber (Boston, 1981), p. 303.

28. For a discussion of the unsolved legal problem
in comparable worth see L. Gasaway, Comparable Worth: A
Post-Gunther Overview," Georgetown Law Journal 69 (June
1981), pp. 1142-43. Also see testimony of W. Newman and
C. Owens, "Race and Sex-Based Wage Discrimination is
Illegal," prepared for the U.S. Commission on Civil
Rights Consultation on Comparable Worth, 7 June 1984 and
paper submitted by R. E. Williams to the commission,
"Comparable Worth: Legal Perspectives and Precedents."

29. Mosher is discussing problems for federal public
administrators that have resulted from their new
responsibilities of heavy third-party contact and
interaction in the course of implementation of programs.
See F. Mosher, "The Changing Responsibilities and Tactics
of the Federal Government," Public Administration Review
40 (November/December 1980), p. 548.

30. W.H. Lambright, Governing Science and Technology
(New York, 1976), p. 29.

31. See H. Ingram's interesting discussion of
bargaining among intergovernmental actors in "Policy
Implementation Through Bargaining," Public Policy 25
(Fall 1977), pp. 499-526. Also R. Elmore's work that
contributed to the analytic framework in Chapter 3,
"Organizational Models of Social Programs," Public Policy
26 (Spring 1978), pp. 185-228. Matthew Holden, Jr.,
identifies the limitation of bargaining for
administrative agencies when dealing with constituencies,
other agencies, or interest groups, especially over
jurisdictional matters. He describes "bureaucratic
imperialism" whereby administrative politicians seek
power through a favorable balance of external or internal
constituencies by strategically organizing and protecting
agency jurisdiction. His work is a classic portrayal of
the organizational pathologies to which administrative
agencies are subject. M. Holden, Jr., "'Imperialism' in
Bureaucracy," in Bureaucratic Power in National Politics,
2d ed., ed. F.E. Rourke (Boston, 1972), pp. 197-214.

32. G.T. Sulzner, "Politics, Labor Relations and
Public Personnel Management," Policy Studies Journal 11
(December 1982), pp. 278-89.

33. S.M. Neuse, "A Critical Perspective on the
Comparable Worth Debate," Review of Public Personnel
Administration 3 (Fall 1982), p. 16.

34. Ibid., p. 17.

35. D.E. Klinger, "Variables Affecting the Design of
State and Local Personnel Systems," in Public Personnel
Administration, ed. S. Hays and R. Kearney (Englewood
Cliffs, NJ, 1983), pp. 17-26.

36. E. Johansen, "From Social Doctrine to Implementation: The Case of Comparable Worth," _Policy Studies Review_ (Summer 1984, forthcoming.)

37. E. Johansen, "Comparable Worth: Surveying the Controversy," p.11.

38. R. Marshall and B. Paulin, "The Employment and Earnings of Women: The Comparable Worth Debate," a paper prepared for the U.S. Commission on Civil Rights Consultation on Comparable Worth, 7 June 1984.

39. E. Johansen, "Comparable Worth: Surveying the Controversy," p. 11.

Appendix A
Chronology of Events
Relating to Comparable Worth's Adoption
in the Several States

1951   Massachusetts adopts statute prohibiting discrimination in wage rates based on sex (Sec. 105A, Ch. 149, General Laws of Mass., as last amended by Ch. 131, L. 1980, effective Aug. 3, 1980).

1955   Arkansas adopts Sec. 81-624, Arkansas Statutes, requiring "every employer in the state to pay employees equal compensation for equal services ...." and forbidding discrimination on the basis of sex in wages paid "to female employees performing work comparable to that performed by male employees." Enacted by Act 361, L. 1955.

1961   (President's Commission on Status of Women, PCSW, is established.)

1962   (Attorney General Robert Kennedy issues 1834 AG ruling relative to the president's ability to forbid selection by sex in federal employment.)

        (President Kennedy issues Executive Order 10988, 17 January 1962, granting federal employees the right to bargain collectively with government agencies.)

1963   (Equal Pay Act adopted, forbidding wage differentials based on sex for workers protected by the Fair Labor Standards Act.)

        PCSW report, American Woman, published, as was Betty Friedan's The Feminine Mystique.)

1964   (Civil Rights Act of 1964 adopted.)

1965   Maine adopts equal pay statute that forbids

employers to pay lesser rates to employees of
either sex for "comparable work on jobs which
have comparable requirements relating to skill,
effort, and responsibility" (Sec. 628, Title 26,
Ch. 7, Maine Revised Statutes, last amended by
Ch. 150, Laws 1965). Oklahoma and West Virginia
pass laws prohibiting discrimination between the
sexes in pay for comparable work, or work of
comparable character.

1966   Georgia, Kentucky, and Maryland pass statutes
with comparable character of work language.

(National Organization for Women, NOW, founded.)

1967   (President Johnson issues Executive Order 11246,
prohibiting employment discrimination based on
race, color, religion, sex, or national origin by
first- and second-tier government contractors.)

(Wisconsin state government reorganized.)

Nebraska passes equal pay statute. Cook cites
that Nebraska's FEP law uses comparable work
language in its policy section.

(NOW adopts "Bill of Rights.")

1968   Women's Equity Action League, WEAL, founded.

(California and Colorado state governments
reorganized.)

1969   Idaho adopts statute with comparable work
language.

(Delaware, Florida, Maryland, and Massachusetts
state governments reorganized.)

("Women's Rights" used in presidential task force
title: "President's Task Force on Women's Rights
and Responsibilities")

1970   (Hearings begin on ERA.)

1971   (WEAL Women's Legal Defense Fund created.)

(The Improvement of State Legislatures--The First
Five Years of Eagleton's Legislative Center,
published in October.)

(Arizona, Georgia, Maine, and North Carolina
state governments reorganized.)

1972   (Center for Women Policy Studies, CWPS, founded.)

(Center for Law and Social Policy, CLASP, creates Women's Rights Project.)

(Equal Employment Opportunity Act of 1972 passed.)

(Women's Lobby formed.)

(Kentucky and Virginia state goverments reorganized.)

(Title IX, ERA, Title IV, and Civil Rights Act amended.)

1973   State of Washington initiates its first comparable worth study.

(South Dakota state government reorganized.)

1974   (County of Washington, Oregon discharges female guards. Alberta Gunther et al. file suit under Title VII, 42 U.S.C. seeking back pay and other relief.)

(Coalition of Labor Union Women, CLUW, formed nationally.)

Tennessee passes statute with comparable character of work language.

1975   State employee unions in Maine and Minnesota commence studies of pay disparity.

(Wellesley College Conference on Occupational Segregation, Center on Women in Higher Education and the Professions.)

(International Women's Year, Mexico City, adopts equal work for equal value amendment.)

(NOW's national convention passes resolution calling for the overturn of the Bennett Amendment.)

1976   (NOW national convention endorses aid in unionization of women workers.)

Idaho passes law requiring a job evaluation system as its wage-setting method.

(Washington publishes Phase II of its comparable

worth study.)

1977 (Eleanor Holmes Norton new chair, Equal Employment Opportunity Commission, EEOC.)

(Reorganization Plan of EEOC introduced in Congress.)

(Communications Workers of America endorses comparable worth.)

(Women's Conference, Houston, "National Plan of Action.")

State of Wisconsin "passes legislation requiring equal pay for work of equivalent skills and responsibility to eliminate pay disparity between occupational groups"

(Christensen v. The University of Northern Iowa, 563 F.2d 355, 8th Cir. 1977.)

(Jointly sponsored Connecticut "Upward Mobility Law" passes; no appropriation.)

(Connecticut Department of Administrative Services reorganized.

Connecticut Permanent Commission on the Status of Women publishes study (a joint venture with Connecticut State Employees Association) concerning sex discrimination in clerical work, "Clerical Work: A Manual for Change."

1978 (Reorganization Plans Nos. 1 and 2, 1978, pass U.S. Congress. Civil Service Reform Plan adopted, as is plan for restructuring of EEOC.)

New Jersey State Women's Commission forms "Commission on Sex Discrimination in the Statutes."

Committee on Pay Equity, Washington, begins planning of Pay Equity Conference.

(Lemons v. City and County of Denver, 620 F.2d 228, 10th Cir. D.Col. 1978.)

Office of Women and Work (OWW), Michigan Department of Labor, conducts study of civil service employees regarding possible sex segregation. Contracts Arthur D. Young to conduct study. Uses CETA funds.

NOW convention endorses comparable worth and labor activism.

1979   CLUW resolution for comparable worth, fourth national convention.

Conference on Pay Equity, Washington, National Committee on Pay Equity formed.

AFL-CIO endorses comparable worth at annual convention.

Minnesota completes job evaluation study.

National Academy of Sciences issues interim report on job evaluation.

Connecticut authorizes pilot study of classification system.

City of San Jose and AFSCME commission studies.

1980   Massachusetts amends statute re discrimination.

Alaska inserts comparable worth language into its Fair Employment Practices.

EEOC holds hearings on job segregation.

Lemons v. City and County of Denver, cert. denied 101 S.Ct. 244 (1980).

AFSCME commissions a Temple University study of state employment in Pennsylvania.

IUE v. Westinghouse, 631 F.2d 1094 (3d Cir.).

Connecticut commences second one-year study of classification system.

1981   California adopts comparable worth legislation.

Connecticut funds four-year study of classification system.

Supreme Court rules in Gunther v. County of Washington 452 U.S. 161 (1981) that Title VII is broader than Equal Pay Act.

Michigan State Employees Association clerical unit files charges of sex discrimination with State Department of Civil Rights and EEOC against State of Michigan.

National Council for Research on Women, umbrella group for twenty-one centers, founded.

1982   Illinois legislature authorizes study.

Nebraska Women's Legislative Caucus forms task force on pay equity to stimulate action.

Kentucky passes legislative resolution authorizing study.

CSEA and State of New York negotiate comparable worth study.

Hawaii, Kentucky, and Illinois pass resolutions for comparable worth studies.

1983   Maine sends out requests for proposals to consultants for comparable worth study.

Minnesota appropriates $21.8 million for pay equity increases.

The Eagleton Institute coordinates December 1983 conference for women legislators, San Diego, California.

New Mexico appropriates $3.3 million for lowest-paid state employees.

California extends its 1981 law, creates Commission on Status of Women task force on comparable worth.

S. 1900, Pay Equity Act of 1983, introduced in Congress by Senator Alan Cranston.

Illinois passes legislation for pilot study with comparable worth standards.

Iowa adopts comparable worth policy and job evaluation study.

Kentucky appropriates $14,000 for a job evaluation study.

Massachusets appropriates $7,500 for a job evaluation study.

Missouri requires report regarding comparable worth policies.

Montana adopts comparable worth goal.

Nevada authorizes study.

Oregon appropriates $300,000 for job evaluation study.

Washington appropriates $1.5 million for equity adjustments.

1984   Legislation introduced in Congress: H.R. 4599, Federal Employees' Pay Equity Act of 1984, and H.Con. Res. 244, Pay Equity Resolution of 1984.

New Jersey appropriates $300,000 for two-year study. Legislation establishes a pay equity policy and a task force to monitor job evaluation study.

Virginia enacts preliminary authorization for a classification study.

Minnesota legislation establishes comparable worth standards for local government.

House Concurrent Resolution 244, Pay Equity Resolution of 1984.

Local governments with comparable worth activities: Colorado Springs, CO; Virginia Beach, VA; Bellevue, WA; Renton, WA; Seattle, WA; Los Gatos, CA; Long Beach, CA; Burlington, VT; Princeton, MN; Los Angeles, CA; Spokane, WA; Green Bay, WI; San Mateo, CA; San Jose, CA; Hennepin County, MN; Belmont, CA.

Sources for Appendix A

Cook, A. (1983) Comparable Worth: The Problem and State's Approaches to Wage Equity. Manoa: University of Hawaii at Manoa, Industrial Relations Center.

Bureau of National Affairs. (1981) The Comparable Worth Issue: A BNA Special Report. Washington, DC: BNA.

National NOW Times, 1967-1978.

Peirce, N.R. (1975) "State-Local Report/ Structural Reform of Bureaucracy Grows Rapidly," National Journal 7:502-8.
Rothchild, N. (1984) "Overview of Pay Equity Initiatives, 1974-1984." Paper prepared for the U.S. Commission on Civil Rights Consultation on Comparable Worth," June 6-7, Washington, DC.

Bibliography

Abcarian, G., ed. (1971) American Political Radicalism.
    Waltham, MA: Xerox College Publishers.
Abcarian, G. (1971) "Romantics and Renegades--Political
    Defection and the Radical Left," Journal of Social
    Issues 27 (January):123-39.
Abney, G. (1983) "The Governor as Chief Administrator,"
    Public Administration Review 43 (January/Febru-
    ary):40-49.
Advisory Commission on Intergovernmental Relations.
    (1981) The Condition of Contemporary Federalism:
    Conflicting Theories and Collapsing Constraints.
    A-78. Washington, DC: ACIR.
Advisory Commission on Intergovernmental Relations.
    (1981) The Federal Role in the Federal System: The
    Dynamics of Growth: An Agenda for American Federal-
    ism. Restoring Confidence and Competence. Washing-
    ton, DC: ACIR.
Advisory Commission on Intergovernmental Relations.
    (1977) The States and Intergovernmental Aids: The
    Intergovernmental Grant System: An Assessment and
    Proposed Policies. A-59. Washington, DC: ACIR.
Alexander, H.E. (1976) Campaign Money: Reform and Reality
    in the States. New York: Free Press.
Allan, P., and Rosenberg, S. (1978) "New York City's
    Approach to Civil Service Reform: Implications for
    State and Local Governments," Public Administration
    Review 38 (November/December):579-84.
American Federation of State, County, and Municipal
    Employees, et al., vs. State of Washington, et al.,
    Docket No. C 82-465T, Daily Labor Report (Washing-
    ton, DC: Bureau of National Affairs), December 15,
    1983.
American Society for Personnel Administration and Ameri-
    can Compensation Association. (1981) Elements of
    Sound Base Pay Administration. Berea, OH: ASPA.
Arnott, C. (1973) "Feminists and Anti-Feminists as 'True
    Believers,'" Sociology and Social Research 57

143

(April):300-6.

Arrington, T.S., and Kyle, P.A. (1978) "Equal Rights Amendment Activists in North Carolina," _Signs_ 3 (Spring):666-80.

Ash, R. (1972) _Social Movements in America_. New York: Markham.

Baer, J.A. (1978) _Chains of Protection_. Westport, CT: Greenwood Press.

Bailey, S. (1980) "Improving Federal Governance," _Public Administration Review_ 40 (November/December):548-52.

Bardach, E. (1977) _The Implementation Game: What Happens after a Bill Becomes a Law_. Cambridge: MIT Press.

Bardach, E. (1980) "On Designing Implementable Programs." In _Pitfalls of Analysis_, ed. G. Majone and E.S. Quade, pp. 138-58. New York: Wiley.

Bardach, E. (1972) _The Skill Factor in Politics: Repealing the Mental Commitment Laws in California_. Berkeley: University of California Press.

Barbash, F. (1984) "State Courts Emerge as Protectors of Individual Rights: A Role Reversal from the Warren Years," _Washington Post National Weekly_, April 16, p. 29.

Barbash, F., and Sawyer, K. (1984) "A New Era of 'Race Neutrality' in Hiring? Justice Department Says Memphis Ruling Reopens Many Affirmative Action Plans," _Washington Post National Weekly_, June 25, p. 32.

Barone, M., and Ujifusa, G. (1984) _The Almanac of American Politics_. Washington, DC: National Journal.

Barringer, F. (1984) "A Bureaucratic Brawl Splits the EEOC," _Washington Post National Weekly_, March 26, pp. 30, 31.

Bates, M., and Vail, R. (1976) "Job Evaluation and Equal Employment Opportunity: A Tool for Compliance—A Weapon for Defense," _Employee Relations Law Journal_ 1 (Spring):535-46.

Beckman, N. (1981) "Intergovernmental Relations: The Future Is Now," _Public Administration Review_ 41 (November/December):701-10.

Bell, D. (1972) "On Meritocracy and Equality," _Public Interest_ 29 (Fall):29-68.

Bellace, J.R. (1980) "A Foreign Perspective." In _Comparable Worth: Issues and Alternatives_, ed. E.R. Livernash, pp. 137-72. Washington, DC: Equal Employment Advisory Council.

Bellack, A.O. (1984) "Comparable Worth: A Practitioner's View." Paper prepared for the U.S. Commission on Civil Rights Consultation on Comparable Worth, June 6-7, Washington, DC.

Bellack, A., Bates, M., and Glasner, D. (1983) "Job Evaluation: Its Role in the Comparable Worth Debate," _Public Personnel Management_ 12 (Winter):418-24.

Beller, A.H. (1980) "The Effect of Economic Conditions on the Success of Equal Employment Opportunity Laws: An

Application to the Sex Differential in Earning,"
Review of Economics and Statistics 62
(August):379-87.

Bellone, C.J. (1982) "Structural vs. Behavioral Change:
The Civil Service Reform Act of 1978," Review of
Public Personnel Administration 2 (Spring):59-67.

Berch, B. (1982) The Endless Day: The Political Economy
of Women and Work. New York: Harcourt Brace Jovano-
vich.

Bernstein, L. (1982) "Chairwoman Finds Labor Background
Useful in New Role," Hartford Courant, November 29,
pp. B1, 2.

Beyle, T.L. (1979) "Governors' Views on Being Governor,"
State Government, Summer, pp. 103-9.

Bibb, R., and Form, W. (1977) "The Effects of Industry,
Occupations, and Sex Stratification on Wages in Blue
Collar Markets," Social Forces 55 (June):974-96.

Biggart, N.W. (1977) "The Creative-Destructive Process of
Organizational Change: The Case of the Post
Office," Administrative Science Quarterly 22 (Sep-
tember):410-23.

Biloon, S. (1979) "Collective Bargaining in Connecticut:
Some Good News and Some Bad News," Intergovernmental
Personnel Notes (Connecticut Office of Personnel
Management), July-August, pp. 17-20.

Black, V. (1974) "The Erosion of Legal Principles in the
Creation of Legal Policies," Ethics 84 (January):93-115.

Blau, F.D., and Jusenius, C.L. (1976) Economists'
Approaches to Sex Segregation in the Labor Market:
An Appraisal." In Women and the Workplace: The
Implications of Occupational Segregation, ed. M.
Blaxall and B. Reagan, pp. 181-99. Chicago: Uni-
versity of Chicago Press.

Blaxall, M., and Reagan, B., eds. (1976) Women and the
Workplace: The Implications of Occupational Segregation. Chicago: University of Chicago Press.

Blumrosen, R. (1981) "Pay Equity Cases Can Be Won Blumrosen Says," Convention News (issued during the American Nurses Association convention, June 29).

Blumrosen, R.G. (1979) "Wage Discrimination, Job Segregation, and Title VII of the Civil Rights Act of
1964," University of Michigan Journal of Law Reform
12 (Spring):397-502.

Blumrosen, R.G. (1979) "Wage Discrimination, Job Segregation and Women Workers," Women's Rights Law Reporter
6 (Fall/Winter):19-57.

Boles, J.K. (1979) The Politics of the Equal Rights
Amendment. New York: Longman.

Boulding, K. (1976) "Comment I." In Women and the Workplace: The Implications of Occupational Segregation,
ed. M. Blaxall and B. Reagan. Chicago: University
of Chicago Press.

146

Brady, D., and Tedin, K. (1976) "Ladies in Pink: Religion and Political Ideology in the Anti-ERA Movement," Social Science Quarterly 56 (March):564-75.

Bridges, W.P., and Berk, R.A. (1978) "Sex, Earnings, and the Nature of Work: A Job-Level Analysis of Male-Female Income Differences," Social Science Quarterly 58 (March):553-65.

Briggs v. City of Madison, 536 F. Supp. 435 (1982), 442-50.

Brown, S.J. (1980) "The Comparable Worth Issue--A Title VII Pandora's Box?" National Law Journal, July 26, p. 27.

Bucknell, S. (1980) "The Connecticut Story on Objective Job Evaluation." In Manual on Pay Equity: Raising Wages for Women's Work, ed. J.A. Grune, pp. 122-28. Washington, DC: Committee on Pay Equity, Conference on Alternative State and Local Policies.

Bucknell, S. (1980) "Testimony on Behalf of Connecticut's Commission on the Status of Women,"in Hearings before the U.S. Equal Employment Opportunity Commission, April 28-30.

Buford, J.A., Jr., and Norris, D.R. (1980-81) "A Salary Equalization Model: Identifying and Correcting Sex-Based Salary Differences," Employee Relations Law Journal 6 (Winter):406-21.

Bunzel, J.H. (1982) "To Each According to Her Worth?" Public Interest, Spring, pp. 77-93.

Bureau of National Affairs. (1981) The Comparable Worth Issue: A BNA Special Report. Washington, DC: BNA.

Burr, S.G. (1981) "Women and Work." In The Women's Annual, ed. B. Haber, pp. 303-21. Boston: G.K. Hall.

"A Business Group Fights 'Comparable Worth.'" (1980) Business Week, November 10, pp. 100, 105.

Canada. Human Rights Commission. (1980) Equal Pay for Male and Female Employees Who Are Performing Work of Equal Value. Ottawa: Human Rights Commission.

Canada. Human Rights Commission. (1980) Methodology and Principles for Applying Section 11 of the Canadian Human Rights Act. Ottawa: Human Rights Commission.

Caplow, T. (1954) The Sociology of Work. Minneapolis: University of Minnesota Press.

Carden, M.L. (1965) "The Experimental Utopia in America," Daedalus, Spring, pp. 403-18.

Carden, M.L. (1974) The New Feminist Movement. New York: Russell Sage Foundation.

Carson, C.B. (1971) "The Mind of the Reformer." In American Political Radicalism, ed. G. Abcarian. Waltham, MA: Xerox College Publishers.

Celarier, M. (1981) "The Paycheck Challenge of the Eighties--Comparing Job Worth," Ms., March, pp. 38, 43-44.

Chafe, W.H. (1972) The American Woman: The Changing

Social, Economic and Political Roles, 1920-1970.
New York: Oxford University Press.

Chapman, J.R. (1983) "Policy Centers: An Essential Resource." In Women in Washington: Advocates for Public Policy, vol. 7, ed. I. Tinker, pp. 177-90. Beverly Hills: Sage.

Christensen v. The University of Northern Iowa, 563 F.2d 355 (8th Cir. 1977).

Clark, P.B., and Wilson, J.Q. (1961) "Incentive Systems: A Theory of Organizations," Administrative Science Quarterly 6 (September):129-66.

Clausen, R. (1979) "Women and Their Organizations." In Women Organizing: An Anthology, ed. B. Cummings and V. Schuck. Metuchen, NJ: Scarecrow Press.

Cobb, R.W., and Elder, C.D. (1972) Participation in American Politics: The Dynamics of Agenda-Building. Boston: Allyn and Bacon.

Cobb, R., Ross, J.-K., and Ross, M.H. (1976) "Agenda Building as a Comparative Political Process," American Political Science Review 70 (March):126-38.

Cohodas, N. (1983) "Women Shift Focus on Hill to Economic Equity Issues," Congressional Quarterly 41 (April):781-89.

Colburn, D.R., and Sher, R.K. (1980) Florida's Gubernatorial Politics in the 20th Century. Tallahassee: University Presses of Florida.

Comparable Worth Project Newsletter. January 1981-Summer 1983. Vols. 1-3.

Connecticut. General Assembly. (1979) "Report of the Upward Mobility Committee to the Legislature." Hartford: State of Connecticut.

Connecticut. Permanent Commission on the Status of Women. (1977) "Clerical Work: A Manual for Change." Hartford: State of Connecticut.

Connecticut State Employees Association (CSEA) v. State of Connecticut, U.S. District Court, District of Conn., Civil Action H-79-197, February 25, 1983.

Connecticut State Employees Association (CSEA) v. State of Connecticut, Intervention complaint filed by AFSCME, July 1982, in U.S. District Court, District of Conn., Civil Action H-79-197.

Cook, A. (1980) "Collective Bargaining as a Strategy for Achieving Equal Opportunity and Equal Pay." In Equal Employment Policy for Women, ed. R. Ratner, pp. 53-78. Philadelphia: Temple University Press.

Cook, A. (1983) Comparable Worth: The Problem and States' Approaches to Wage Equity. Manoa: University of Hawaii at Manoa, Industrial Relations Center.

Cook, A. (1983) "Comparable Worth, Recent Developments in Selected States," IRRA Proceedings (Meeting of Industrial Relations Research Association, March 16-18).

Cook, A. (1968) "Women and American Trade Unions," Annals
of the American Academy of Social and Political Sci-
ence 375 (January):124-32.
Corcoran, M., and Duncan, G.J. (1979) "Work History,
Labor Force Attachment, and Earnings Differences
between the Races and Sexes," Journal of Human
Resources 14 (Winter):3-20.
Council of State Governments. (1982) The Book of the
States, 1980-81. Lexington, KY: CSG.
Council of State Governments. (1983) The Book of the
States, 1982-83. Lexington, KY: CSG.
"The Court Strains to Make Work: Why Did it Have to
Decide the Seniority Case At All?" (1984) Editorial,
New York Times, June 14, p. A22.
Couturier, J.J. (1983) "Civil Service Reform Issues in
State Government." In Public Personnel Administra-
tion: Problems and Prospects, ed. S.W. Hays and R.C.
Kearney, pp. 278-304. Englewood Cliffs, NJ: Pren-
tice-Hall.
Couturier, J.J., and Schick, R.P. (1983) "The Second Cen-
tury of Civil Service Reform: An Agenda for the
1980s." In Public Personnel Administration: Prob-
lems and Prospects, ed. S.W. Hays and R.C. Kearney,
pp. 311-29. Englewood Cliffs, NJ: Prentice-Hall.
Craig, B. (1982) "The Legislative Veto: Its Implications
for Administration and the Democratic Process."
Ph.D. diss., University of Connecticut.
Cummings, B., and Schuck, V., eds. (1979) Women Organiz-
ing: An Anthology. Metuchen, NJ: Scarecrow Press.
Daniels, M., and Darcy, R. (1984) "As Times Goes By: The
Arrested Diffusion of the Equal Rights Amendment."
Unpublished paper.
Daniels, M., Darcy, R., and Westphal, J.W. (1982) "The
ERA Won--At Least in the Opinion Polls," PS 15
(Fall):578-84.
Daniels, M., and Regens, J.L. (1981) "Physicians' Assis-
tants as a Health Care Delivery Mechanism: Incidence
and Correlates of State Authorization," Policy Stud-
ies Journal 19 (Special Issue):242-50.
Davis, C., and West, J. (1983) "Jobs, Dollars, and Gen-
der: An Analysis of the Comparable Worth Issue in
Urban Areas." Paper delivered at American Society
for Public Administration Annual Meeting, New York.
Davis, C.E., and West, J.P. (1983) "Support for Affirma-
tive Action in a Metropolitan Bureaucracy." In Public Personnel Administration, ed. S. Hays and R.
Kearney, pp. 262-73. Englewood Cliffs, NJ: Pren-
tice-Hall.
Derthick, M. (1972) New Towns In-Town: Why a Federal Pro-
gram Failed. Washington,DC: Urban Institute.
Diamond, I. (1977) Sex Roles in the Legislature. New
Haven: Yale University Press.
Dresang, D.L. (1982) "Diffusion of Civil Service Reform:

The Federal and State Governments," Review of Public Personnel Administration 2 (Spring):35-47.

Dresang, D.L. (1978) "Public Personnel Reform: A Summary of State Government Activity," Public Personnel Management 7 (September/October):298-94.

Dye, T.R., and Zeigler, L.H. (1971) The Irony of Democracy. Belmont, CA: Duxbury Press.

East, C. (1983) "Newer Commissions." In Women in Washington: Advocates for Public Policy, vol. 7, ed. I. Tinker, pp. 35-48. Beverly Hills: Sage.

Edelman, M. (1967) Symbolic Uses of Politics. Urbana: University of Illinois Press.

"The EEOC--It is 'a changing.'" (1978) Mission (Equal Employment Opportunity Commission) 6:1.

Ehrenhalt, A. (1983) "Power Shifts in State Capitols as Professional Lawmakers Take Over Leadership Spots: Conservative Democrats Weakened," Congressional Quarterly 41 (September):1767-69.

Elazar, D. (1966) American Federalism: A View from the States. New York: Crowell.

Elazar, D. (1969) "The American Partnership: The Next Half Generation." In The Politics of American Federalism, ed. D. Elazar, pp. 221-25. Boston: Heath.

Elmore, R. (1978) "Organizational Models of Social Programs," Public Policy 26 (Spring):185-228.

England, P. (1984) "Explanations of Job Segregation and the Sex Gap in Pay." Paper prepared for the U.S. Commission on Civil Rights Consultation on Comparable Worth, June 6-7, Washington, DC.

England, P., Chassie, M., and McCormack, L. (1982) "Skill Demands and Earnings in Female and Male Occupations," Sociology and Social Research 66 (January):147-68.

Eyde, L.D. (1983) "Evaluating Job Evaluation: Emerging Research Issues for Comparable Worth Analysis," Public Personnel Management 12 (Winter):425-44.

Eyestone, R. (1977) "Confusion, Diffusion, and Innovation," American Political Science Review 71 (June):441-47.

Farnquist, R., Armstrong, D.R., and Strausbaugh, R.P. (1983) "Pandora's Worth: The San Jose Experience," Public Personnel Management 12 (Winter):358-68.

Ferber, M.A., and Kordick, B. (1978) "Sex Differentials in the Earnings of Ph.D.s," Industrial and Labor Relations Review 31 (January):227-38.

Field, J. (1975) "The Coalition of Labor Union Women," Political Affairs 54 (March):3-12.

Flick, R. (1983) "New Feminism and the World of Work," Public Interest, Spring, pp. 33-44.

"Focus on Women." (1982) Connecticut Magazine, January, pp. 85-125.

Foner, P.S. (1979) Women and the American Labor Movement. New York: Free Press.

Foster, G.D. (1981) "Law, Morality, and the Public Servant," Public Administration Review 41 (January/February):29-34.

Fox, D.M. (1981) "Reorganizing State Government," Bureaucrat 10 (Fall):69-70.

Fredland, R. (1983) "Valuing Work: Complications--Contradictions--Compensation," Public Personnel Management 12 (Winter):461-66.

Freeman, J. (1979) "Resource Mobilization and Strategy: A Model Formalizing Social Movement Through Organization Action." In The Dynamics of Social Movements, ed. M. Zald and J.D. McCarthy, pp. 170-89. Cambridge, MA: Winthrop.

Freeman, J. (1975) The Politics of Women's Liberation. New York: McKay.

Freeman, J. (1973) "Tyranny of Structurelessness," Ms., July, pp. 76-78, 86-89.

Freeman, J. (1983) Women: A Feminist Perspective. New York: Mayfield.

Friss, L. (1982) "Equal Pay for Comparable Worth: Stimulus for Future Civil Service Reform," Review of Public Personnel Administration 2 (Summer): 37-48.

Garnett, J.G. (1980) Reorganizing State Government: The Executive Branch. Boulder, CO: Westview Press.

Gasaway, L.N. (1981) "Comparable Worth: A Post-Gunther Overview," Georgetown Law Journal 69 (June):1123-69.

Gates, M.J. (1976) "Occupational Segregation and the Law." In Women and the Workplace: The Implications of Occupational Segregation, ed. M. Blaxall and B. Reagan, pp. 61-73. Chicago: University of Chicago Press.

Gelb, J., and Klein, E. (1983) Women's Movements: Organizing for Change in the 1980's. Washington, DC: American Political Science Association.

Gelb, J., and Palley, M.L. (1982) Women and Public Policies. Princeton: Princeton University Press.

Gelb, M. (1979) "Litigating Comparable Worth Cases," National Lawyers Guild Women's Newsletter, February, pp. 4-5.

General Accounting Office. (1976) "The EEOC Has Made Limited Progress in Eliminating Employment Discrimination." Washington, DC: GAO (September).

Gergen, K.J. (1968) "Assessing the Leverage Points in the Process of Policy Formation." In The Study of Policy Formation, ed. R.A. Bauer and K.J. Gergen, pp. 181-203. New York: Free Press.

Gerson, E. (1982) "Shackled to Past: Pay Equity Eludes Women," Hartford Courant, October 11, p. A17.

Gertzog, I.N., and Simard, M.M. (1981) "Women and the 'Hopeless' Congressional Candidates, American Politics Quarterly 9 (October):449-66.

Gilliam, D. (1984) "Oyez- Oyez-" Washington Post, June 14, p. 1.

Ginzberg, E. (1979) _Good Jobs, Bad Jobs, No Jobs_. Cambridge: Harvard University Press.

Ginzberg, E. (1977) "The Job Problem," _Scientific American_, November, pp. 1-9.

Glazer, N. (1980) "Affirmative Discrimination: Where Is It Going?" _International Journal of Comparative Sociology_ 20, 1-2:14-30.

Gold, M. (1983) _A Dialogue on Comparable Worth_. Ithaca: ILR Press.

Goodin, J.M. (1983) "Working Women: The Pros and Cons of Unions." In _Women in Washington: Advocates for Public Policy_, vol. 7, ed. I. Tinker, pp. 140-64. Beverly Hills: Sage.

Goodman, E. (1983) "The Case for Being Unrealistic," _Project on the Status and Education of Women_ (Association of American Colleges) 2 (Spring):11.

Goodman, E. (1978) "Earning Less for Women's Work," _Washington Post_, October 16.

Goodman, E. (1977) "Equal Pay for Work of Equivalent Value," _Washington Post_, May 21, p. A-11.

Goodman, E. (1983) "ERA and Pay Equity: Unfinished Business for American Women," _Hartford Courant_, June 10, p. B11.

Gray, V. (1973) "Innovation in the States: A Diffusion Study," _American Political Science Review_ 67 (December): 1174-86.

Gray, V. (1973) "Rejoinder to 'Comment' by J.L. Walker," _American Political Science Review_ 67 (December):1192-93.

Green, D.H. (1981-82) "An Application of the Equal Pay Act to Higher Education," _Journal of College and University Law_ 8:203-18.

Gregory, R.G., and Duncan, R.C. (1981) "The Relevance of Segmented Labor Market Theories: The Australian Experience of the Achievement of Equal Pay for Women," _Journal of Post-Keynesian Economics_ 3 (Spring): 403-28.

Griffiths, M.W. (1976) "Can We Still Afford Occupational Segregation? Summary Remarks." In _Women and the Workplace: The Implications of Occupational Segregation_, ed. M. Blaxall and B. Reagan, pp. 7-14. Chicago: University of Chicago Press.

Griffiths, M.W. (1966) "Women Are Being Deprived Legal Rights by the Equal Employment Opportunity Commission," _Congressional Record_, House, June 20, pp. 13689-94.

Gross, E.C. (1968) "Plus Ca Change . . .? The Sexual Structure of Occupations Over Time," _Social Problems_ 1, 2:198-208.

Grumm, J.G. (1971) "The Effects of Legislative Structure on Legislative Performance." In _State and Urban Politics: Readings in Comparative Public Policy_, ed. R.I. Hofferbert and I. Sharkansky, pp. 298-322.

Boston: Little, Brown.

Grune, J.A., ed. (1980) Manual on Pay Equity. Washington, DC: Committee on Pay Equity, Conference on Alternative State and Local Policies.

Grune, J.A., and Reder, N. (1983) "Pay Equity: An Innovative Public Policy Approach to Eliminating Sex-Based Wage Discrimination," Public Personnel Management 12 (Winter):395-403, 405-7.

Gunderson, M. (1978) "The Influence of the Status and Sex Composition of Occupations on the Male-Female Earnings Gap," Industrial and Labor Relations Review 31 (January):217-26.

Gunther v. County of Washington, 452 U.S. 161 (1981).

Gusfield, J.R., ed. (1970) Protest, Reform and Revolt: A Reader in Social Movements. New York: Wiley.

Haener, D. (1980) "Letter to the Women's Bureau." In Manual on Pay Equity: Raising Wages for Women's Work, ed. J.A. Grune, pp. 66-67. Washington, DC: Committee on Pay Equity, Conference on Alternative State and Local Policies.

Hargrove, E.C. (1975) The Missing Link: The Study of Implementation of Social Policy. Washington, DC: Urban Institute.

Hartmann, H., and Treiman, D. (1983) "Notes on NAS Study of Equal Pay for Jobs of Equal Value," Public Personnel Management 12 (Winter): 404-17.

Hays, S.W., and Kearney, R.C., eds. (1983) Public Personnel Administration: Problems and Prospects. Englewood Cliffs, NJ: Prentice-Hall.

Heard, A. (1966) "Reform: Limits and Opportunities." In State Legislatures in American Politics, ed. A. Heard, pp. 154-62. Englewood Cliffs, NJ: Prentice-Hall.

Heard, A., ed. (1966) State Legislatures in American Politics. Englewood Cliifs, NJ: Prentice-Hall.

Hedblom, M.K. (1983) Women and American Political Organizations and Institutions. Washington, DC: American Political Science Association.

Henle, P. (1980) "The Distribution of Earned Income among Men and Women, 1958-77," Monthly Labor Review 103 (April):3-10.

Hershey, M.R., and West, D.M. (1983) "Single Issue Politics: Prolife Groups and the 1980 Senate Campaign." In Interest Group Politics, ed. A.J. Cigler and B.A. Loomis, pp. 31-59. Washington, DC: Congressional Quarterly Press.

Hershey, R.D. (1983) "Women's Pay Fight Shifts to 'Comparable Worth,'" New York Times, November 1, p. A15.

Holden, M., Jr. (1972) "'Imperialism' in Bureaucracy." In Bureaucratic Power in National Politics, 2d ed., ed. F.E. Rourke, pp. 197-214. Boston: Little, Brown.

Holsendolph, E. (1984) "Skills, Not Bias, Seen as Key for

Jobs," New York Times, July 3, p. 5.
Hoppe, L.D. (1977) "Agenda Setting Strategies: Pollution Policy." Cited in C.S. Jones, An Introduction to the Study of Public Policy, 2d ed., p. 39. Duxbury, MA: Duxbury Press.
Howard, S. (1983) "CSEA Eyes November Vote as First Step in Resurgence," Hartford Courant, October 27, p. B2.
Hunter, M. (1984) "Candidates' Relations Testify for Equitable Pay Proposal," New York Times, April 4.
Huwa, R., and Rosenthal, A. (1977) Politicians and Professionals: Interactions between Committee and Staff in State Legislatures. New Brunswick, NJ: Rutgers University Press.
Hyde, A.C., and Shafritz, J.M. (1983) "Position Classification and Staffing." In Public Personnel Administration, ed. S. Hays and R. Kearney, pp. 99-117. Englewood Cliffs, NJ: Prentice-Hall.
Ingersoll, F.S. (1983) "Former Congresswomen Look Back." In Women in Washington: Advocates for Public Policy, vol. 7, ed. I. Tinker, pp. 191-208. Beverly Hills: Sage.
Ingram, H. (1977) "Policy Implementation through Bargaining: The Case of Federal Grants-in-Aid," Public Policy 25 (Fall):499-526.
International Labour Organization. (1949) Equal Remuneration for Men and Women Workers for Work of Equal Value. Report V(1). Geneva: International Labour Office.
International Labour Organization. (1975) 'Equal Remuneration': General Survey by the Committee of Experts on Applications of Conventions and Recommendations. Report III (Part 4B). Geneva: International Labour Office.
International Union of Electrical, Radio and Machine Workers, AFL-CIO-CLC et al. v. Westinghouse Electric Corporation, 631 F.2d 1094 (3d Cir. 1980); cert. denied, 452 U.S. 967 (1981).
Jacob, H. (1966) "Dimensions of State Politics." In State Legislatures in American Politics, ed. A. Heard, pp. 5-36. Englewood Cliffs, NJ: Prentice-Hall.
Jacobson, C.J. (1980) "New Challenges for Women Workers," AFL-CIO American Federationist, April, pp. 1-8.
Jaffe, L.L. (1965) Judicial Control of Administrative Action. Boston: Little, Brown.
Jennings, M.K., and Niemi, R. (1981) Generations and Politics. Princeton: Princeton University Press.
Jennings, M.K., and Zeigler, H. (1971) "The Salience of American State Politics." In State and Urban Politics: Readings in Comparative Public Policy, ed. R.I. Hofferbert and I. Sharkansky, pp. 59-82. Boston: Little, Brown.
Jewell, M.E. (1966) "The Political Setting." In State

Legislatures in American Politics, ed. A. Heard, pp. 70-97. Englewood Cliffs, NJ: Prentice-Hall.

Jewell, M.E., and Olson, D.M. (1982) *American State Political Parties and Elections*. Homewood, IL: Dorsey Press.

Johansen, E. (1984) "Comparable Worth: Surveying the Controversy," *Bureaucrat* 13 (Spring):8-11.

Johansen, E. (1984) "From Social Doctrine to Implementation: The Case of Comparable Worth," *Policy Studies Review* (Summer, forthcoming).

Johansen, E. (1984) "Instructive but Disappointing: Johansen's Response to Stahl," *Bureaucrat* 13 (Spring):15.

Johansen, E. (1984) "Managing the Revolution: The Case of Comparable Worth," *Review of Public Personnel Administration* 4 (Spring):14-27.

Kallen, D.B.P., Kosse, G.B., Wagenaar, H.C., Kloprogge, J.J.J., and Vorbeck, M. (1982) *Social Science Research and Public Policy-Making*. London: Unwin.

Kantor, R. (1976) "Presentation VI." In *Women and the Workplace: The Implications of Occupational Segregation*, ed. M. Blaxall and B. Reagan, pp. 282-91. Chicago: University of Chicago Press.

Kaufman, H. (1981) "Fear of Bureaucracy: A Raging Pandemic," *Public Administration Review* 41 (January/February):1-9.

Kaufman, H. (1977) *Red Tape: Its Origins, Uses, and Abuses*. Washington, DC: Brookings Institution.

Kay, W.F., and Stevens, M.C. (1982) "Potential Impact of Concept of Comparable Worth on Public Sector Bargaining," *National Public Employment Reporter* 4 (March):25-36.

Keefe, W.J. (1966) "The Functions and Powers of the State Legislatures." In *State Legislatures in American Politics*, ed. A. Heard, pp. 37-69. Englewood Cliffs, NJ: Prentice-Hall.

Killingsworth, V. (1981) "Labor: What's a Job Worth?" *Atlantic*, February, pp. 10, 11, 16, 17.

King, D. (1983) "Oldest State Comparable Worth Battle Continues," *Comparable Worth Project Newsletter*, Summer, pp. 8-9.

Kirkpatrick, J.J. (1974) *Political Woman*. New York: Basic Books.

Kirschten, R. (1984) "The Reagan Reelection Campaign Hopes 1984 Will Be the Year of the Women," *National Journal* 16:1082-85.

Klapper, M.J. (1975) "The Limitations of the Equal Pay Principle: A Critical Essay," *Industrial and Labor Relations Forum* 11 (Spring): 65-105.

Klinger, D.E. (1979) "Changing Role of Personnel Management in the 1980s," *Personnel Administrator*, September, pp. 41-48.

Klinger, D.E. (1981) "Political Influences on the Design

of State and Local Personnel Systems," *Review of Public Personnel Administration* 1 (Summer):1-10.

Klinger, D.E. (1983) "Variables Affecting the Design of State and Local Personnel Systems." In *Public Personnel Administration*, ed. S. Hays and R. Kearney, pp. 17-26. Englewood Cliffs, NJ: Prentice-Hall.

Klinger, D.E., and Nalbandian, J. (1978) "Personnel Management by Whose Objectives?" *Public Administration Review* 38 (July/August):366-72.

Kramer, K.W. (1982) "Seeds of Success and Failure: Policy Development and Implementation of the 1978 Civil Service Reform Act," *Review of Public Personnel Administration* 2 (Spring):5-20.

Krauthamer, N. (1976) "The Taxability of Title VII 'Back Pay' Awards," *Taxes* 54 (June):332-38.

Lanham, E. (1963) *Administration of Wages and Salaries*. New York: Harper and Row.

Lanham, E. (1955) *Job Evaluation*. New York: McGraw-Hill.

Lasswell, H., and Kaplan, A. (1950) *Power and Society*. New Haven: Yale University Press.

"Lawmaker and Mrs. Schlafly Clash over Equal Pay Issue." (1984) *New York Times*, April 15.

Leach, D.E. (1979) "An Emerging Concept: Equal Pay for Work of Equal Value." In *The Prentice-Hall EEO Compliance Manual*, pp. 247-50. Englewood Cliffs, NJ.

Leach, D.E., and Werley, E.L. (1983) "Comparable Worth, Job Evaluation and Wage Discrimination: The Employer Approaches Wage Gap Issues of the 1980s," *Public Personnel Management* 12 (Winter):345-57.

Lemons v. *City and County of Denver*, 620 F.2d 228 (10th Cir.); cert. denied, 101 S.Ct. 244 (1980).

Lepper, M.M. (1983) "Affirmative Action: A Tool for Effective Personnel Management." In *Public Personnel Administration*, ed. S. Hays and R. Kearney, pp. 217-45. Englewood Cliffs, NJ: Prentice-Hall.

Lepper, M.M. (1976) "The Status of Women in the U.S., 1976: Still Looking for Justice and Equity," *Public Administration Review* 36 (September-October):365-69.

Levine, C.H. (1981) "Hidden Hazards of Retrenchment," *Bureaucrat* 10 (Fall):4-5.

Levine, C., and Nigro, F. (1975) "The Public Personnel System: Can Juridical Administration and Manpower Management Coexist?" *Public Administration Review* 35 (January/February):98-107.

Levy, Claudia (1980) "'Comparable Worth' May be Rights Issue of '80s," *Washington Post*, October 13, Bus. sec., p. 3.

Lewin, T. (1984) "A New Push to Raise Women's Pay," *New York Times*, January 1, p. C1.

Lewis, E. (1977) *American Politics in a Bureaucratic Age: Citizens, Constituents, Clients and Victims*. Cambridge, MA: Winthrop.

Livernash, E.R., ed. (1980) *Comparable Worth: Issues and*

Alternatives. Washington, DC: Equal Employment
Advisory Council.

Lloyd, C., and Niemi, B.T. (1979) _The Economics of Sex
Differentials_. New York: Columbia University Press.

Lockard, D. (1976) "A Mini-Symposium--The Strong Governorship: Status and Problems," _Public Administration
Review_ 36 (January/February):90-98.

Lockard, D. (1968) _Toward Equal Opportunity: A Study of
State and Local Anti-Discrimination Laws_. New York:
Macmillan.

Loomis, B.A., and Cigler, A.J., eds. (1983) _Interest
Group Politics_. Washington, DC: Congressional Quarterly Press.

Lorber, L.L., and Kirk, J.R. (1983) "A Status Report on
the Theory of Comparable Worth: Recent Developments
in the Law of Wage Discrimination," _Public Personnel
Management_ 12 (Winter):332-44.

Lowi, T. (1964) "American Business, Public Policy Case
Studies and Political Theory," _World Politics_ 16
(July):677-715.

Lowi, T. (1969) _The End of Liberalism_. New York: Norton.

Lowi, T. (1972) "Four Systems of Policy, Politics and
Choice," _Public Administration Review_ 32 (July-August):298-310.

Lowi, T. (1971) _The Politics of Disorder_. New York: Norton.

Lynn, L.E.J. (1980) _Designing Public Policy_. Santa
Monica, CA: Goodyear.

Lynn, N.B., and Vaden, R.E. (1979) "Bureaucratic Response
to Civil Service Reform," _Public Administration
Review_ 39 (July/August):333-43.

Lytle, C.W. (1946) _Job Evaluation Methods_. New York:
Ronald Press.

Marshall, R., and Paulin, B. (1984) "The Employment and
Earnings of Women: The Comparable Worth Debate."
Paper prepared for the U.S. Commission on Civil
Rights Consultation on Comparable Worth, June 6-7,
Washington, DC.

McCombs, P. (1984) "The Commission's 'Okay' Person,"
Washington Post National Weekly, February 27, pp.
32-33.

McDowell, G.L. (1983) "Reagan and Affirmative Action."
Paper delivered at the Southern Political Science
Association meeting, Birmingham.

McLenna, B.N. (1982) "Sex Discrimination in Employment
and Possible Liabilities of Labor Unions: Implications of _Washington_ v. _Gunther_," _Labor Law Journal_
33 (January):26-35.

Mead, M., and Kaplan, F.B., eds. (1965) _American Woman:
The Report of the U.S. President's Commission on the
Status of Women_. New York: Scribner's.

Meeker, S. (1981) "Equal Pay, Comparable Worth, and Job
Evaluation," _Yale Law School Journal_ 90

(January):657-80.

Merry, G.B. (1984) "Citizen-Initiated Legislation May Be on the Ballot in 19 States." Christian Science Monitor, May 15.

Milkovich, G.T. (1981) "The Male-Female Pay Gap: Need for Reevaluation," Monthly Labor Review, April, pp. 42-43.

Milkovich, G.T., and Broderick, R. (1982) "Pay Discrimination: Legal Issues and Implications for Research," Industrial Relations 21, 3:309-17.

Miller, A.R., Treiman, D.J., Cain, P.S., and Roos, P.A., eds. (1980) Work, Jobs and Occupation: A Critical Review of the Dictionary of Occupational Titles. Report of the Committee on Occupational Classification and Analysis to the U.S. Department of Labor. Washington, DC: National Academy Press.

Miller, E. (1979) "Consensus: Equal Pay for Comparable Work," Personnel 56 (September/October):4-9.

Mills, C.W. (1959) The Sociological Imagination. New York: Oxford University Press.

Mills, D.Q. (1979) "Human Resources in the 1980s," Harvard Business Review, July, pp. 154-62.

Millsap, M.A. (1983) "Sex Equity in Education." In Women in Washington: Advocates for Public Policy, vol. 7, ed. I. Tinker, pp. 91-119. Beverly Hills: Sage.

Moe, R.C. (1982) "A New Hoover Commission: A Timely Idea or Misdirected Nostalgia?" Public Administration Review 42 (May/June):270-77.

Moe, T. (1981) "A Broader View of Interest Groups," Journal of Politics 43 (May):531-43.

Moe, T. (1980) The Organization of Interests. Chicago, University of Chicago Press.

Moore, M.L., and Johnson, C.G. (1977) "Bona Fide Training Programs: The Legal Basis," Labor Law Journal 28 (February):120-24.

Morehouse, S.M. (1981) State Politics, Parties and Policy. New York: Holt, Rinehart and Winston.

Morehouse, S.M. (1973) "The State Political Party and the Policy-Making Process," American Political Science Review 67 (March):60.

Moroney, J.R. (1979) "Do Women Earn Less Under Capitalism?" Economic Journal 8-9 (September):601-13.

Mosher, F. (1980) "The Changing Responsibilities and Tactics of the Federal Government," Public Administration Review 40 (November/December):541-48.

Mosher, F.C. (1978) "The Public Service in Temporary Society." In Classics of Public Administration, ed. J.M. Shafritz and A.C. Hyde, pp. 373-90. Oak Park, IL: Moore.

Moynihan, D.P. (1970) "The Professionalization of Reform." In Protest, Reform and Revolt: A Reader in Social Movements, ed. J.R. Gusfield, pp. 245-57. New York: Wiley.

Nalbandian, J., and Klinger, D. (1981) "The Politics of Public Personnel Administration: Towards Theoretical Understanding," _Public Administration Review_ 41 (September/October):541-49.

National Employment Law Project. (1973) _Legal Services Manual for Title VII Litigation._ New York: National Employment Law Project.

"National Conference Resolutions." (1975, 1978) _National NOW Times,_ November.

National NOW Times (1975) November.

Nelson, B. (1978) "Setting the Public Agenda: The Case of Child Abuse." In _The Policy Cycle,_ ed. J. May and A.B. Wildavsky. Beverly Hills: Sage.

Nelson, B.A., Opton, E.M., and Watson, T.E. (1980) "Wage Discrimination and the 'Comparable Worth' Theory in Perspective," _University of Michigan Journal of Law Reform_ 13 (Winter):231-301.

Nelson, B.A., Opton, E.M., Jr., Wilson, T.E. (1980-81) "Wage Discrimination and Title VII in the 1980s: The Case Against 'Comparable Worth,'" _Employee Relations Law Journal_ 6 (Winter):380-405.

Neuse, S.M. (1982) "A Critical Perspective on the Comparable Worth Debate," _Review of Public Personnel Administration_ 3 (Fall):1-20.

Newland, C.A. (1983) "A Mid-term Appraisal--The Reagan Presidency: Limited Government and Political Administration," _Public Administration Review_ 43 (January/February):1-22.

Newland, C.A. (1976) "Public Personnel Administration: Legalistic Reforms v. Effectiveness, Efficiency and Economy," _Public Administration Review_ 36 (September/October):529-37.

Newman, W. (1983) "Statement to Equal Pay Joint Committee," _Public Personnel Management_ 12 (Winter):382-89.

Newman, W. (1978) "Statement" in _Hearings_ of the Subcommittee on Employment Opportunities of the House Committee on Education and Labor, November 29.

Newman, W., and Owens, C. (1984) "Race- and Sex-Based Wage Discrimination is Illegal." Testimony before the U.S. Commission on Civil Rights Consultation on Comparable Worth, June 6-7, Washington, DC.

Newman, W., and Wilson, C.W. (1981) "The Union Role in Affirmative Action," _Labor Law Journal,_ June, pp. 323-42.

Niemi, A.W., Jr. (1977) "Sexist Earning Differences: The Cost of Female Sexuality," _American Journal of Economics and Sociology_ 36 (January):33-40.

Noll, R.G. (1971) "The Behavior of Regulatory Agencies," _Review of Social Economy_ 29 (March):15-19.

Norris, B. (1983) "Comparable Worth, Disparate Impact, and the Market Rate Salary Problem: A Legal Analysis and Statistical Application," _California Law Review_

71 (March):730-75.

Nowlan, J.D. (1976) The Politics of Higher Education. Urbana: University of Illinois Press.

O'Kelly, C. (1979) "The 'Impact' of Equal Employment Legislation on Women's Earnings: Limitations of Legislative Solutions to Discrimination in the Economy," American Journal of Economics and Sociology 38 (October):418-30.

Oldfield, J.D. (1976) "A Case Study on the Impact of Public Policy Affecting Women," Public Administration Review 36 (July/August):385-89.

Olson, M. (1968) Logic of Collective Action. New York: Schocken.

O'Neill, J., and Braum, R. (1981) Women and the Labor Market: A Survey of Issues and Policies in the U.S. Washington, DC: Urban Institute.

O'Neill, W.L. (1969) Everyone Was Brave: A History of Feminism in America. New York: New York Times Book Company.

Oppenheimer, V.K. (1970) The Female Labor Force in the United States: Demographic and Economic Factors Governing Its Growth and Changing Composition. Westport, CT: Greenwood Press.

Owens, C. (1981) Pay Equity for Women: A Special Report. New York: McGraw-Hill.

Packwood, R. (1984) "Discrimination Aided," New York Times, April 20, p. A27.

Paradix, A.A., and Paradix, G.D. (1983) The Labor Almanac. Littleton, CO: Libraries Unlimited.

Parcel, T.L., and Mueller, C.W. (1983) Ascription and Labor Markets: Race and Sex Differences in Earnings. New York: Academic Press.

Parcel, T.L., and Mueller, C.W. (1983) "Occupational Differentiation, Prestige, and Socioeconomic Status," Work and Occupations (Beverly Hills: Sage) 10 (February).

Parsons, T. (1942) "Age and Sex in the Social Structure of the U.S.," American Sociological Review 7 (October):604-16.

Patten, T.H., Jr. (1978) "Pay Discrimination Lawsuits: The Problems of Expert Witness and the Effects of the Discovery Process," Personnel 55 (November/December):27-35.

Pauly, G.M. (1982) "Comparable Worth vs. Prevailing Rates: The Conflict between Politics and Sound Public Administration," Western City, January, pp. 10-13.

"Paying Women What They're Worth," QQ 3 (Spring 1983):1-3.

Pear, R. (1984) "Administration May Challenge Equal Pay Rule: Top Officials Press Case Over Women's Suit," New York Times, January 22, pp. 1, 16.

Pear, R. (1983) "G.M. Agrees to Pay $42 Million to End

160

Case on Job Bias," New York Times, October 19, pp. 1, 21.

Peirce, N.R. (1984) "Comparable Pay--Comparable Dedication?" Hartford Courant, April 29.

Peirce, N.R. (1975) "Employment Report/ Public Employee Unions Show Rise in Membership, Militancy," National Journal 7:1239-49.

Peirce, N.R. (1981) "New Panels to Move Quickly to Help Reagan Unbend the Federal System," National Journal 13:785-88.

Peirce, N.R. (1975) "State-Local Report/ Structural Reform of Bureaucracy Grows Rapidly," National Journal 7:502-8.

Perlez, J. (1984) "Women, Power, and Politics," New York Times Magazine, June 24, pp. 23-26, 28, 30-31, 72, 76.

Perrow, C. (1979) "The Sixties Observed." In The Dynamics of Social Movements, ed. M.N. Zald and J.D. McCarthy, pp. 192-211. Cambridge, MA: Winthrop.

Peterson, C., and Causey, M. (1984) "Can the GOP 'Create Disorder'?: A Reagan Official's Plan to Use 'Comparable Worth,'" Washington Post National Weekly, June 11, p. 11.

Peterson, E. (1983) "The Kennedy Commission." In Women in Washington: Advocates for Public Policy, vol. 7, ed. I. Tinker, pp. 21-34. Beverly Hills: Sage.

Pidgeon, M. (1937) Women in the Economy of the USA. Washington, DC: Women's Bureau.

Polochek, S.W. (1984) "Women in the Economy: Perspectives on Gender Inequality." Paper prepared for the U.S. Commission on Civil Rights Consultation on Comparable Worth, June 6-7, Washington, DC.

President's Economic Report for 1973. (1973) Weekly Compilation of Presidential Documents, January 30, p. 101.

Pressman, J.L., and Wildavsky, A.B. (1973) Implementation: How Great Expectations in Washington Are Dashed in Oakland. Berkeley: University of California Press.

"Profiles of the 50 States." (1983) Congressional Quarterly 41 (September):1771-1871.

Ramirez, B.C., and Berry, M.F. (1984) "Civil Rights Commission Majority vs. a National Consensus," New York Times, February 26.

Ranney, A. (1973) "The Political Parties: Reform and Decline." In The New American Political System, ed. A. King, chap. 6. Washington, DC: American Enterprise Institute.

Ransone, C.B., Jr. (1982) The American Governorship. Westport, CT: Greenwood Press.

Ratner, R. Steinberg. (1980) Equal Employment Policy for Women. Philadelphia: Temple University Press.

Rawalt, M. (1983) "The Equal Rights Amendment." In Women

in Washington: Advocates for Public Policy, vol. 7,
    ed. I. Tinker, pp. 49-78. Beverly Hills: Sage.
Reichenberg, N.E. (1984) "Labor Relations: Additional
    Comparable Worth Legislation Introduced," IPMA NEWS,
    March, pp. 6-8.
Rein, M. (1976) Social Science and Public Policy. New
    York: Penguin Books.
Remick, H. (1980) "Beyond Equal Pay for Equal Work: Com-
    parable Worth in the State of Washington." In Equal
    Employment Policy for Women, ed. R. Steinberg Rat-
    ner, pp. 405-18. Philadelphia: Temple University
    Press.
Remick, H. (1983) "An Update on Washington State," Public
    Personnel Management 12 (Winter):390-94.
Remick, H. (1982) "The Comparable Worth Controversy." In
    Subcommittees on Human Resources, Civil Service Com-
    pensation and Employee Benefits of the House Commit-
    tee on Post Office and Civil Service, Joint Hearings
    on Pay Equity: Equal Pay for Work of Comparable
    Value, Parts I and II, pp. 1666-83. 97th Cong., 2d
    sess., September 16, 21, 30, and December 2.
Remick, H. (n.d.) "Comparable Worth: Equal Pay for Equal
    Worth." In Collected Papers: Educational Equity
    Issues in Community Colleges, pp. 49-66. Pullman:
    Washington State University.
Remick, H. (1978) "Strategies for Creating Sound, Bias-
    Free Job Evaluation Plans." Paper presented at Sym-
    posium on Job Evaluation and EEO: The Emerging
    Issues, Industrial Relations Counselors, Inc.,
    Atlanta, September 14-15.
"Rights Commission Plans Comparable Worth Study." (1984)
    Public Administration Times, February 1, p. 1.
Risher, H., and Cameron, M. (1981-82) "Pay Decisions:
    Testing for Discrimination," Employee Relations Law
    Journal 7 (Winter):432-53.
Rosen, B., Rynes, S., and Mahoney, T.A. (1983) "Compensa-
    tion, Jobs, and Gender," Harvard Business Review,
    July-August, pp. 170-90.
Rosenthal, A. (1971) The Improvement of State Legisla-
    tures--The First Five Years of Eagleton's Legisla-
    tive Center. New Brunswick, NJ: Rutgers University
    Press.
Rosenthal, A. (1981) Legislative Life: People, Process
    and Performance in the States. New York: Harper and
    Row.
Rosenthal, A., and Huwa, R. (1977) Politicians and Pro-
    fessionals: Interactions between Committee and Staff
    in State Legislatures. New Brunswick, NJ: Rutgers
    University, Center for State Legislative Research
    and Service, Eagleton Institute of Politics.
Rossi, A.S. (1965) "Women in Science: Why So Few?" Sci-
    ence 148 (May):1196-1202.
Rothchild, N. (1984) "Overview of Pay Equity Initiatives,

1974-1984." Paper prepared for the U.S. Commission on Civil Rights Consultation on Comparable Worth, June 6-7, Washington, DC.

Sabatier, P., and Mazmanian, D. (1980) "The Implication of Public Policy: A Framework of Analysis," Policy Studies Journal 8 (Special Issue): 538-40.

Sabato, L. (1978) Goodbye to Good-Time Charlie: The American Governor Transformed. Lexington, MA: Lexington Books.

Sabato, L. (1979) "Governors' Office Careers: A New Breed Emerges," State Government, Summer, pp. 95-102.

Salisbury, R. (1969) "An Exchange Theory of Interest Groups," Midwest Journal of Political Science 13 (February):1-32.

Salisbury, R. (1983) "Interest Groups: Toward A New Understanding." In Interest Group Politics, ed. A.J. Cigler and B.A. Loomis, pp. 354-69. Washington, DC: Congressional Quarterly Press.

Savage, R.L. (1978) "Policy Innovativeness as a Trait of American States," Journal of Politics 40:212-24.

Schattschneider, E.E. (1960) The Semisovereign People. Hinsdale, IL: Dryden Press.

Schick, R.P., and Couturier, J.J. (1977) The Public Interest in Government Labor Relations. Cambridge, MA: Ballinger.

Schlafly, P. (1983) "Equal Pay for Comparable Worth," Woman Constitutionalist, September 24, p. 2.

Schlesinger, J. (1971) "The Politics of the Executive." In Politics in the American States, ed. H. Jacob and K.N. Vines, pp. 222-34. Boston: Little, Brown.

Schuchman, H.L. (1982) "Technology: Women's Work," Graduate Women, November/December. Reprinted, Quarterly (Women's Caucus for Political Science) 9 (April):11-13.

Scott, J.W. (1982) "Mechanization of Women's Work," Scientific American, September, pp.166-87.

Sealander, J.A. (1977) "The Women's Bureau, 1920-1950: Federal Reaction to Female Wage Earning." Ph.D. diss., Duke University.

Seidman, H. (1980) Politics, Position, and Power. New York: Oxford University Press.

Seifer, N., and Wertheimer, B. (1979) "New Approaches to Collective Power: Four Working Women's Organizations." In Women Organizing, ed. B. Cummings and V. Schuck, pp. 152-220. Metuchen, NJ: Scarecrow Press.

Selznick, P. (1949) TVA and the Grass Roots. Berkeley: University of California Press.

"Senate Confirms E.H. Norton." (1977) Mission (Equal Employment Opportunity Commission) 5:4.

"Sex-based Wage Discrimination and the Bennett Amendment Issue in International Union of Electrical Workers v. Westinghouse Electric Corp.: The Case for Comparable Worth." (1981) American University Law

Review 30 (Winter): 547-77.

Shabecoff, P. (1977) "Phone Union Will Ask Woman Job Upgrade," _New York Times_, February 19.

Shafritz, J.M., Hyde, A.C., and Rosenbloom, D.H. (1981) _Personnel Management in Government_. 2d ed. New York: Marcel Dekker.

Sharkansky, I. (1969) "The Utility of Elazar's Political Culture: A Research Note," _Polity_ 2 (Fall):66-83.

Sherrill, R. (1965) "Florida's Legislature: The Pork Chop State of Mind," _Harper's_, November, pp. 82-97.

Simchak, M. MacLeod. (1971) "Equal Pay in the U.S.," _International Labor Review_ 103 (June):541-57.

Simpson, P. (1983) "Washington--the Fight for Pay Equity," _Working Woman_, April, pp. 70-77.

Skok, J.E. (1980) "Federal Funds and State Legislatures: Executive-Legislative Conflict in State Government," _Public Administration Review_ 40 (November/December):561-67.

Smith, L. (1978) "The EEOC's Bold Foray into Job Evaluation," _Fortune_, September 11, pp. 58-64.

Spelfogel, E.J. (1981) "Equal Pay for Work of Comparable Value: A New Concept," _Labor Law Journal_ 32 (January):30-9.

Stanfield, R.L. (1984) "All the Way to the Supreme Court: States Make Federalism a Federal Case," _National Journal_ 16:71-74.

Stanway, H.G. (1947) _Applied Job Evaluation_. New York: Ronald Press.

Stavisky, L.P. (1981) "State Legislatures and the New Federalism," _Public Administration Review_ 41 (November/December):717-22.

Steinberg, C. (1981) "Beyond the Days of Wine and Roses: Intergovernmental Management in a Cutback Environment," _Public Administration Review_ 41 (January/February):10-20.

Steinberg, R.J. (1984) "Identifying Wage Discrimination and Implementing Pay Equity Adjustments." Paper prepared for the U.S. Commission on Civil Rights Consultation on Comparable Worth, June 6-7, Washington, DC.

Steinberg, R.J. (1983) "A Want of Harmony: Perspectives on Wage Discrimination." Working Paper 12. Albany: SUNY, Center for Women in Government.

Steinberg, R.J. (1982) "Typical and Alternative Routes to Promotion of Women and Minorities," _Journal of Public and International Affairs_ 3 (Fall/Winter):13-26.

Steinberg, R.J. (1982) _Wages and Hours: Labor and Reform in Twentieth Century America_. New Brunswick, NJ: Rutgers University Press.

Stencel, S. (1981) "Equal Pay Fight," _Editorial Research Reports_ 1 (March 20): 211-28. Washington, DC: Congressional Quarterly.

Stewart, D. (1982) "EEO, Merit and the Political

164

Environment of Public Sector Employment," Policy
Studies Journal 11 (December):290-97.
Stewart, D. (1984) "Managing Competing Claims: An Ethical
Framework for Human Resource Decision-Making," Pub-
lic Administration Review 44 (January/Febru-
ary):14-22.
Stewart, D. (1980) The Women's Movement: Community Poli-
tics in the U.S. New York: Pergamon Press.
Sulzner, G.T. (1982) "Politics, Labor Relations and Pub-
lic Personel Management," Policy Studies Journal 11
(December):279-89.
Sussman, B. (1984) "Most Explanations of the Gender Gap
Don't Hold Up," Washington Post National Weekly,
February 20, p. 36.
Taber, G., and Remick, H. (1978) "Beyond Equal Pay for
Equal Work: Comparable Worth in the State of Wash-
ington." Paper prepared for Conference on Equal Pay
and Equal Opportunity Policy for Women in Europe,
Canada, and the United States, Center for Research
on Women, Wellesley College, Wellesley, MA.
Thomsen, D.J. (1978) "Eliminating Pay Discrimination
Caused by Job Evaluation," Personnel, September-Oc-
tober, pp. 11-22.
Thomsen, D.J. (1979) "Equal but Unequal Pay," Personnel
Journal, August, pp. 515-18.
Thorton, A., and Freeman, D. (1979) "Changes in Sex Role
Attitudes in Women, 1962-1977: Evidence from a Panel
Study," American Sociological Review 44 (Octo-
ber):831-42.
Tinker, I. (1983) "Women Develop Strategies for Influenc-
ing Policy." In Women in Washington: Advocates for
Public Policy, vol. 7, ed. I. Tinker, pp. 163-64.
Beverly Hills: Sage.
Tinker, I. (1983) "Women Organize for Change." In Women
in Washington: Advocates for Public Policy, vol. 7,
ed. I. Tinker, p. 45. Beverly Hills: Sage.
Tinker, I., ed. (1983) Women in Washington: Advocates for
Public Policy, vol. 7. Beverly Hills: Sage.
Treiman, D.J. (1979) Job Evaluation: An Analytic Review.
Washington, DC: National Academy of Sciences.
Treiman, D.J., and Hartmann, H.I., eds. (1981) Women,
Work, and Wages: Equal Pay for Jobs of Equal Value.
Washington, DC: National Academy Press.
Treiman, D., and Terrell, K. (1975) "Women, Work and
Wages -- Trends in the Female Occupational Struc-
ture." In Social Indicator Models, ed. K. Land and
S. Spilerman, pp. 157-99. New York: Russell Sage
Foundation.
Tucker, M. (1978) Reorganization of the EEOC. Boston:
Intercollegiate Case Clearing House.
U.S. Congress. House. Subcommittees on Human Resources,
Civil Service Compensation and Employee Benefits of
the Committee on Post Office and Civil Service.

(1982) <u>Joint Hearings on Pay Equity: Equal Pay for Work of Comparable Value, Parts I and II.</u> 97th Cong., 2d sess., September 16, 21, 30, and December 2.

U.S. Department of Commerce, Bureau of the Census. (1982) <u>Statistical Abstract of the United States, 1982-83.</u> Washington, DC: Government Printing Office.

U.S. Department of Commerce, Bureau of the Census. (1983) <u>Statistical Abstract of the United States.</u> Washington, DC: Government Printing Office.

U.S. Department of Labor, Women's Bureau. (1963) <u>Economic Indicators Relating to Equal Pay.</u> No. 9. Washington, DC: Women's Bureau.

U.S. Department of Labor, Women's Bureau. (1973) "Memorandum for Ms. Grace Ferill, Regional Director, Boston" (Subject: "Funding of Commissions on Status of Women"; April 16). Washington, DC: Women's Bureau.

U.S. Department of Labor, Women's Bureau. (1969) "Statutory Commissions on the Status of Women" (background paper, limited distribution; October). Washington, DC: Women's Bureau.

U.S. Equal Employment Opportunity Commission. (1981) <u>Hearings, Job Segregation and Wage Discrimination.</u> (Hearings held in Washington, DC, April 28-30, 1980.) Washington, DC: Government Printing Office.

Wagenaar, H.C. (1982) "A Cloud of Unknowing: Social Science Research in a Political Context." In <u>Social Science Research and Public Policy Making: A Re-Appraisal,</u> ed. D.B.P. Kallen, G.B. Kosse, H.C. Wagenaar, J.J.J. Kloprogge,and M. Vorbeck, pp. 22-31. London: Unwin.

Wahlke, J.C. (1966) "Organization and Procedure." In <u>State Legislatures in American Politics,</u> ed. A. Heard, pp. 126-53. Englewood Cliffs, NJ: Prentice-Hall.

Walker, D.B. (1981) <u>Toward a Functioning Federalism.</u> Cambridge, MA: Winthrop.

Walker, J.L. (1973) "Comment: Problems in Research on the Diffusion of Policy Innovations," <u>American Political Science Review</u> 67 (December):1186-91.

Walker, J.L. (1969) "The Diffusion of Innovations among the Several States," <u>American Political Science Review</u> 63:880-99.

Walker, J.L. (1977) "Setting the Agenda in the U.S. Senate: A Theory of Problem Selection," <u>British Journal of Political Science</u> 7 (October):423-45.

Walters, R. (1975) "Reform Ripples Reaching Labor," <u>National Journal</u> 7:149.

Wamsley, G.L., and Zald, M.N. (1973) <u>The Political Economy of Public Organizations.</u> Bloomington: Indiana University Press.

"Washington Loses Sex Bias Suit," <u>New York Times,</u> September 19, 1983.

Wegener, E. (1980) "Does Competitive Pay Discriminate?" Personnel Administration 25 (May):38-66.

Welch, S., and Thompson, K. (1980) "The Impact of Federal Incentives on State Policy Innovation," American Journal of Political Science 24 (November):715-29.

Wermiel, S. (1981) "High Court Looks at Women's Pay in Dispute on 'Comparable Worth,'" Wall Street Journal May 14, sec. 2, p. 1.

Wermiel, S. (1981) "Women May Sue on Pay-Bias Claims in Unequal Jobs, High Court Rules, 5 to 4," Wall Street Journal, June 9, p. 4.

Wertheimer, B. (1976) We Were There: The Story of Working Women in America. New York: Pantheon Books.

West, J.P. (1982) "Merit, Bilateralism, Equity and Reform: An Attitudinal Assessment," Journal of Public and International Affairs 3 (Fall/Winter):63-77.

West, J.P. (1981) "Public Sector Collective Bargaining and Merit: Accommodation or Conflict?" Paper presented at American Society for Public Administration meeting, Hartford, CT.

Williams, R.E. (1984) "Comparable Worth: Legal Perspectives and Precedents." Paper prepared for the U.S. Commission on Civil Rights Consultation on Comparable Worth, June 6-7, Washington, DC.

Williams, R.E., and McDowell, D.S. (1980) "The Legal Framework." In Comparable Worth: Issues and Alternatives, ed. E.R. Livernash, pp. 197-250. Washington, DC: Equal Employment Advisory Council.

Williamson, J. (1981) "Equal Pay for Work of Comparable Value," Working Woman, January, pp. 10,16.

Willis, N.D., and Associates. (1980) "Objective Job Evaluation Pilot Study." Hartford: State of Connecticut.

Willis, N.D., and Associates. (1974, 1976) State of Washington Comparable Worth Study. Seattle: Norman D. Willis and Associates.

Wilson, C. (1980) "The IUE's /International Union of Electrical, Radio and Machine Workers of America/ Approach to Comparable Worth." In Manual on Pay Equity: Raising Wages for Women's Work, ed. J.A. Grune, pp. 89-90. Washington, DC: Committee on Pay Equity, Conference on Alternative State and Local Policies.

Wilson, J.Q. (1973) Political Organizations. Boston: Basic Books.

Winslow, M.N. (1951) Women at Work. Minneapolis: University of Minnesota Press.

Withorn, A. (1976) "The Death of CLUW," Radical America 10 (March/April):47-51.

Wolf, W., and Rosenfeld, R. (1978) "Sex Structure of Occupations and Job Mobility," Social Forces 56 (March):823-44.

"The Women Who Changed the South. A Memory of Fannie Lou

Hamer." (1977) <u>Mission</u> (Equal Employment Opportunity Commission) 5:6.

Wright, D.S. (1982) <u>Understanding Intergovernmental Relations</u>. 2d ed. Monterey: Brooks/Cole.

Wright, D.S., and Hebert, F.T. (1980) <u>State Administrators' Opinions on Administrative Change, Federal Aid, Federal Relationships</u>. Washington, DC: ACIR.

Zald, M., and McCarthy, J.D., eds. (1979) <u>The Dynamism of Social Movements</u>. Cambridge, MA: Winthrop.

Zippo, M. (1981) "Equal Pay for Comparable Work," <u>Personnel</u> 58 (November-December);4-10.

Index

19-20, 64

Hargrove, E. C., 101
Hartmann, Heidi, 12, 43
Hawaii, 84
Hay Associates, 15, 107
Hills, Carla, 31
Hobby, Oveta Culp, 31
Hudson, Betty, 60
Huwa, R., 77
Hyde, A. C., 103

Idaho, 83, 84, 87
Illinois, 84, 87
"Inside-access" model, 57,
    59, 60
Intergovernmental Person-
    nel Act of 1970, 103
International Labour
    Office, 14, 31
International Labour Org-
    anization, 31, 41
International Union of
    Electrical Workers, 43
International Women's Year
    Conference, 42
Iowa, 84

Jarvis-Gann initiative
    (Proposition 13), 78
Job evaluation, 1 3, 12-
    15, 18, 22, 54, 84,
    85, 87, 88, 89, 103,
    107, 120, 122, 126,
    127

Kennedy, John F., 32
Kentucky, 83, 84, 86, 87,
    88
King, Debby, 62, 63
King, Edward J., 85

Labeling, 57, 63, 67
Lambright, W. H., 126
Lathrop, Julia, 30
Lee, Eleanor, 106
Legislators, women, 34,
    57, 77, 78, 80, 85,
    89, 111, 121, 122
    See also Beck, Audrey
Legislatures, 73-78, 105,
    111, 126
    professionalism of, 73,

75-78, 79, 80, 92,
    105, 111, 114
Lowi, T., 52-55, 66

Maine, 83, 84, 87
Maine State Employees
    Association, 87
Manual on Pay Equity,
    43-44
Marshall, Ray, 127
Maryland, 83, 84, 87, 88
Maryland Classified Em-
    ployees Association,
    88
Massachusetts, 83-86
Mazmanian, D., 110, 111,
    114
Merit, 3, 16-17, 103-4,
    126
Merit Systems Protection
    Board, 16
Michigan, 31, 84
Minnesota, 84, 106, 107-9,
    121
Minnesota Council on the
    Economic Status of
    Women, 107, 108
Missouri, 84
Montana, 31, 84
Mosher, F., 125
Movements. See Feminist
    movement; Pay equity
    movement; Women's
    rights movement;
    Social movements
Muller v. Oregon, 39, 40

National Academy of
    Sciences, 11-12, 18,
    43
National Committee for
    Equal Pay, 31
National Committee on Pay
    Equity, 43-44
National Council for Re-
    search on Women, 43
National Labor Relations
    Board, 120, 126
National Labor Relations
    Act of 1935, 13
National Organization for
    Women, 34-35, 40,
    41-42

Tanner, Jack E., 109
Taylor, Frederick W., 12
Tedin, K., 131
Tennessee, 83, 84, 85, 86, 87
Terrell, Sylvia, 62
Thompson, K., 103
Tianti, Betty, 61, 62, 63
Tinker, Irene, 42
Title IV, Civil Rights Act of 1964, 36
Title VII, Civil Rigths Act of 1964, 1, 3, 18, 19, 20, 21, 33, 35, 39, 43, 44, 64, 74
Treiman, D., 12, 13, 14, 43

Unionists, women, 27, 39-42, 44, 61-65
Unions, 39-42
Unions, public sector, 86, 87, 88-89, 92, 103, 108, 111, 113, 114, 115, 120, 121, 126. See also Unionists, women
United Auto Workers, 40
United Farm Workers, 41
U.S. Children's Bureau, 30
U.S. Citizens Advisory Council on the Status of Women, 37-38
U.S. Civil Service Commission, 16, 18
U.S. Commission on Civil Rights, 120
U.S. Department of Justice, 120
U.S. Equal Employment Opportunity Commission, 11, 17-19, 22, 34, 36, 37, 43, 120
U.S. Interdepartmental Committee on the Status of Women, 37
U.S. Office of Government Employment, EEOC, 18

U.S. Office of Personnel Management, 16
U.S. Office of Policy Implementation, EEOC, 18
U.S. Supreme Court, 18, 20-21, 36-39, 55, 64, 120, 122, 125
U.S. Treasury Department, 13
U.S. Women's Bureau, 29-32, 37, 43
University of Minnesota, 108
Upward Mobility Program (Connecticut), 60-61

Virginia, 84

Wagner Act, 13
Walker, J. L., 57, 79
Warren, Earl, 76
Washington, 19-20, 36, 41, 55, 61-62, 64, 73, 84, 106-7, 109, 120-23, 124
Waters, Barbara, 64
Welch, S., 79, 104
West, J. P., 110-11, 114, 115
West Virginia, 83, 84, 85, 86, 87
Wildavsky, A. B., 66
Willis, Norman D., and Associates, 19-20, 64
Wisconsin, 84
Women in government, 37-38, 42. See also Legislators, women
Women, Work and Wages, 43
Women's Conference on Pay Equity, 62
Women's Equity Action League, 34, 35
Women's Lobby, 35
Women's rights movement, 3, 8, 36, 122
Women's studies centers, 27

AF